LEADERSHIP

Take Control of your life and Learn what the School Doesn't Teach you.

© Copyright 2020 - All rights reserved.

This document is geared towards providing exact and reliable information with regard to the topic and issue covered. The publication is sold with the idea that the publisher is not required to render accounting, officially permitted or otherwise qualified services. If advice is necessary, legal or professional, a practiced individual in the profession should be ordered. - From a Declaration of Principles which was accepted and approved equally by a Committee of the American Bar Association and a Committee of Publishers and Associations.

In no way is it legal to reproduce, duplicate, or transmit any part of this document in either electronic means or in printed format. Recording of this publication is strictly prohibited, and any storage of this document is not allowed unless with written permission from the publisher. All rights reserved. The information provided herein is stated to be truthful and consistent, in that any liability, in terms of inattention or otherwise, by any usage or abuse of any policies, processes, or directions contained within is the solitary and utter responsibility of the recipient reader.

Under no circumstances will any legal responsibility or blame be held against the publisher for any reparation, damages, or monetary loss due to the information herein, either directly or indirectly. Respective authors own all copyrights not held by the publisher.

The information herein is offered for informational purposes solely and is universal as so. The presentation of the information is without contract or any type of guarantee assurance.

TABLE OF CONTENTS

CHAPTER 1: HOW TO SELL? 4
CHAPTER 2: HOW TO THINK? 13
CHAPTER 3: HOW TO NEGOTIATE 31
CHAPTER 4: HOW TO FACE A FAILURE 42
CHAPTER 5: HOW TO MANAGE TIME 56
CHAPTER 6: HOW TO INVEST MONEY 70
CHAPTER 7: PRINCIPLES OF SUCCESS 86
CHAPTER 8: HOW TO FIND YOUR PASSION 97
CHAPTER 9: HOW TO HANDLE MONEY 115
CHAPTER 10: HOW TO MAKE AN IMPACT 124
CHAPTER 11: HOW TO START A BUSINESS 133
CHAPTER 12: THE IMPORTANCE OF TRAVEL 148
CHAPTER 13: HOW TO COMMUNICATE WELL 157
CHAPTER 14: EMOTIONAL AWARENESS/INTELLIGENCE 170
CHAPTER 15: HOW TO READ A FINANCIAL STATEMENT 181
CHAPTER 16: HOW INCOME TAXES WORKS 195
CONCLUSION 204

Introduction

The unknown is always interesting. How to learn things nobody has ever told you? The art of selling, the motivation, the ways to approach the topic of success. There have been endless works written about these topics and you can choose to follow almost any method imaginable. In the end, the method doesn't matter so much as your ability to follow it, so it is very important to find a method that is simple, easy to understand and very motivational. This book is unique because it teaches you about all the things around the "profession" in the same easy format that a child can use to learn to read! There are so many traits you can learn to help guide your path to success and each of these traits begins with a different letter. By organizing this guide by the letters of the alphabet, it helps you keep track of what you need to do to achieve your goals. As you learn these traits, you can incorporate them into your own life to drive your success.

There are so many successful people in the world that you can learn from. When you study the lives of successful people, you learn about how they achieved their goals. This will help you to determine how you can best achieve your goals too! By studying the life and career of others, you will be able to see how goals are attained and how you can turn your life onto the path you desire. This book will let you inside a world of crucial topics and in the end you will know what to do and motivated to do it.

LEADERSHIP

Chapter 1:

HOW TO SELL?

Your image is your way of dressing, as lights, if you are well-groomed or not, if you dress formally or not, what your clothes say about you and your body language (how you stand, how you walk, etc.).

Your Image is your first impression before the client, the first key to be able to sell big.

Your image sells and sells very well. What's more, before you approach people to try to make a sale, they already saw you from top to bottom, analyzed you, and in a matter of seconds, they formed an idea of you. You didn't have to say anything yet, but they already judged you for better or for worse, and they kept you in their minds in the good or bad zone of their mind that depends on you.

Remember that you are your product and your image is the most important thing to be able to open the dialogue towards a sale. Your image builds trust and if you look your best, people will allow you to get closer to interacting with them. Otherwise prepare yourself for endless rejections: No thanks, I have no change or you are not what I am looking for, thanks.

I have an engineer friend who is a great programmer but he is always unemployed or he doesn't work very long, he is a great computer engineer, but he just doesn't like to wear formal clothes. His favorite clothes for him are his torn black sneakers, his denim pants and his white t-shirts, with that he feels super comfortable and is fine, it is important to feel comfortable while you work, but it does not cover at all the standards of a company of High Prestige.

We know that the image of a company is not only its product, but also its employees. Imagine that you visited the company and I will introduce you to the Systems Engineer dressed like this. What would be your first impression of him? Would you believe me he's an engineer dressed like this? Of course not, right?

Your clothes, sell

The same goes for your way of dressing; it represents not only who you are but what you sell. Imagine that you want to get the best job in the world. Be the Chief or Director of that luxury company and earn the millions that the Chief earns, and you show up for your pants and shirt interview; what do you think, do you

think they would give you the job? Right?

This book was created so that you would be financially free and that you would not spend your whole life receiving a small salary as an employee. But you will earn more, much more, thanks to your skills and attitudes.

For example, I always do my job dressed in a suit and tie and it is not only because it makes me feel comfortable, but it gives me confidence when it comes to selling and confidence is power.

It is as if the client has a special power to feel your vibe, and if you feel good about yourself (looking great and clean), your client will perceive it and will be more attracted to what you sell.

I can swear to you that this advice will do.

It helps me a lot, especially when negotiating a price or closing a deal. It seems like a lie but it is not, the mere fact of wearing a tie or not, makes my client not see me the same.

When I don't wear a tie I look informal and most of the cases have rejected me when offering my product. It seems like magic, I'm just going to put on my tie or bowtie and customers start to fall wanting to hire my services. It's an internal matter; call it that, but dressing well works. It also helps me differentiate myself from the competition; my service is of the highest quality. And my clothing reflects what I do.

It is like the boy who wants to conquer the girl and the first thing that the young lady must pay attention to is the boy's footwear.

If, when he goes on a date with her, he brings the shoes on... he means that he is a clean boy and attentive to details, but if he brings all the careless shoes, that girl is sure to suffer with him. So it is very important that you learn to sell and your clothes sell.

The uniform, let's call it that, or the clothes you wear to represent what you do, will always help you sell more, and give people even more confidence to buy from you.

My musician friends, for example, always wear suits and bow ties, they look super elegant, and on the back of their jackets they embroidered the name of the band they represent. Imagine a Mariachi; you agree that it would not be a complete Mariachi without the corresponding charro suit and hat.I think I cannot imagine and I feel that it would not be to my liking if the Mariachi came to my house, with all my guests, ready for the music and that the Mariachi was dressed in denim.

See what I say they could play and sing very well but without the charro suit, I feel deep down in my heart, like something is missing, don't you think?

When I was a child I loved going to a huge cinema that turned it into a Castle on the Outside! Full of characters and images from your favorite children's movies. It was as if we were in the square of the stars but for children, it was beautiful.

There were even stars on the floor, with the names of the characters, you know that Hollywood type and you could touch them and stand there. I loved going to that cinema, plus there was a huge toy store next to it.

Whenever we arrived, my family and I went into the toy store first, bought an ice cream and went straight to the cinema. Everyone who worked there wore a beanie and a shirt with the "Magic Cinema" logo. Even when there were premieres, some employees dressed like the characters in the movie.

The clothes, the logos, the stars and the form that the cinema has as a castle are pure marketing to attract customers, especially children, and why not? Also to adults and their inner child. ALL THIS SELLS.

Your smile, sells

That's true after dressing, which will make a person like you more; it's a good smile and a reliable greeting. It is very likely that from the beginning people will not shake your hand, but with a good smile and a cheerful and cordial greeting, you can open the dialogue to achieve the sale.

Service and friendliness come first, you don't know how many sellers I see, who know this but don't apply it; First they arrive

LEADERSHIP

with the client, they greet very kindly, smiling and they even tell him a joke, and the client laughs, they like him, but in the end they don't close the sale, they get angry, they talk and they leave very upset saying things under their breath As if the client was not listening. This is very bad, because you leave a bad impression of falsehood to the customer. This then, then thinks: - that seller was not sincere, he was just being nice for me to buy from him, but since I didn't want to, he left very angry, as if buying from him even if I didn't want to, was forced.

And you will have lost a client who perhaps at that time did not need your product, but you do not know if later on, and you will have chased him away with your bad ways. If you act like this, although people may not believe it if they remember you, even if you don't remember them. You as a seller see and talk to millions of people a day, but what a customer remembers most about you, is a bad experience, bad service or a bad sale. Never get mad, don't even speak under your breath if you don't make the sale.

This is a big mistake, you don't know how many times people have said no to me, and a few moments later they say yes.

It has happened to me, that even some clients until the fifth time I have visited them say yes, four times in a row they told me no, and until the 5th time they are already ready to say yes, to buy and buy my service.

People need a product

You have to find the right moment where the customer feels comfortable to buy from you. Never lose faith. You have done your job well and the client will return to you.

For every satisfied customer there are at least 3 new customers to whom this customer will recommend.

But think that for every bad sale you make, there are at least 10 new clients with whom this same client can mention you, but with a bad recommendation to others it is easier for the client to keep a bad recommendation in his mind.

In other words, for every satisfied customer there are 3 possible new sales.

And for every dissatisfied customer there are 10 sales that may not be achieved, just because of a bad attitude or a bad recommendation by that same customer.

This is where you discover who is and who not your potential client is.

I love it because when I give them a test of my talent I can see how people react, in my case I am a musician and my test of talent is to sing a song outdoors before going to the tables to offer my work.

I do it for two things, one to get the attention of the client and know that there is quality in what I sell, and two to discover who can be my best prospects to be my clients. That is to say, to whom I have more possibilities to sell.

It is like throwing a small hook, so that whoever catches it, buys me.

It is a lot of fun, because when singing, at the same time I am analyzing people: as you saw, what kind of music is it that you might like.

As you know I sing from many genres and not all people like the same thing.

Some even hide, like they shrink when I turn to see them. If I see that they cover their ears or look for their cell phone, as if to hide that they don't listen to me, those clients will almost certainly not hire me.

But I also invite them to hire me later, to be my next clients. Normally if they say no, I tell them not to worry, see you at dessert, or to please recommend us, that there in the restaurant we have live music and a family member may be interested.

Some birthday, some baptism etc.

It has happened to me that many of these clients but hire me; bring me a friend and family member who do like my product which is music.

There are even some clients who when I take their eyes off them, I feel that they take confidence and turn to me, they are looking at me, that means that if they like my work.

Some even sing with me, those are the most potential clients that I find.

Offering a little of your talent or product is very good and this is known by Chinese sales experts. You see that when you are in a shopping plaza and you go to see what there is to eat, always in Chinese food, they give you a taste of their sweet and sour chicken, a ball of food on a small stick.

This is a great marketing trick, you are already there, you tried their food and there is a 95% that you buy from them and there are no others for the commitment that you accepted their food.

Also if by it, you were already hungry, that little ball of chicken whet your appetite and your brain says - yes, if you no longer look to eat, eat!

- It is a great trick to sell; all fast food companies have one.

Chapter 2:

HOW TO THINK?

What is system thinking?

There are two fundamental ways in which to respond to an ever-changing world: when events happen, you can react, or, with knowledge of how events work, you can be a participating actor instead of a passive reactor. When a machine breaks down, we respond by trying to fix it. With systems thinking, you begin to develop an ability to predict when and why the machine will break down, therefore giving yourself an edge in terms of strategic planning and decision making.

What is a system? At its most basic, a system is the holistic sum of the interdependent parts which interact with one another to a specific purpose. The crucial point here is that of interaction and interdependence: without these, you merely have a loose collection of parts, not a system. For example, a kitchen in and of itself isn't a system because not all of the parts interact with one another, and it doesn't have one clear overarching purpose;

whereas, an oven is a system, in that all of its working parts must interact in order for it to operate for the purpose of cooking food.

Instead of looking at the surface of things, systems thinking asks that you look deeper into how these structures are created and how they interact with one another. We may be cogs in a machine, as the old saying goes, but we can become cognizant of how those cogs work together, thus building a better machine. The whole is greater than the sum of its parts. Therefore, understanding how systems work is of great advantage to anyone trying to assess and solve challenges. By reframing your perspective – you are no longer looking at a broken machine but a damaged system – you are better equipped to understand that each part is significant in its own way, while the whole working together is significant in the highest way.

There are several key terms to understanding systems thinking, and these are all explored in greater depth throughout the reading. First, the concept of interconnectedness requires that we recognize that all parts are dependent on one another and to the larger system. Think of the term "ecosystem" to illuminate the concept of interconnectedness: this consists of not only the animal life forms but also the plant material, the environmental structure (air quality, water access), the spatial requirements, even the microscopic bacterial components that create good soil and clean water, for example.

When one of these things goes awry, the entire system is compromised. Second, the idea of synthesis is key to systems thinking. Synthesis is,

essentially, recognizing the interconnectedness of a system and being able to study both the whole and its component parts – as well as understanding how they work together. This leads to an understanding of the third key term, emergence: when synthesis is working well, we see an emergence of positive outcomes. Basically, when everything works together seamlessly, we get the Goldilocks effect: it is all "just right." Disruption within a system invariably impedes the emergence of desired goals.

Fourth, to harness the energies of a system, you must get to know how feedback loops work. Top-down styles of thinking and of management no longer respond nimbly and successfully to challenges: if the communication is only going in one direction, then the system gets bogged down in routines, misinformation, and mistrust. Feedback loops can occasionally work against us, as in a reinforcing loop. This is like a recording getting stuck, repeating the same line over and over again. If we are only telling ourselves one story, then it becomes dominant, and the system gets out of balance.

Understanding how feedback loops work is an exercise in old-fashioned rhetoric – understanding cause and effect. When we understand causality, our fifth term is about being able to ascertain how the parts in the system interact with one another – and what emerges from that interaction – then we begin to gain a perspective on the relationships with different elements within the system. This leads to smarter planning and better decisions, ultimately.

Last, the term systems mapping describes the tools that allow us to view how our system is working (or why it is not working and, thus, how to fix it).Thus, systems thinking employ a plethora of diagrams and charts in order to help you look at the system as a whole, understanding how each part affects each other part.

Systems mapping opens up a world of possibilities for problem-solving.

We will look at various archetypes of typical ways in which systems function, and more importantly, how they become dysfunctional over time if we don't examine how the dynamic works. This allows us to look beyond mere events to the patterns of behavior within the system itself that lead up to them. It's a powerful mechanism wherein we become active instead of reactive to events as they occur.

When we examine the enormous problems that we encounter in the world, we must acknowledge that there is no such thing as a simple fix. Often, people will use the phrase "systemic racism," for example, to describe a nefarious problem that isn't limited to one arena of the social sphere, or one isolated event, or even to one time or place or institution. The system itself is arranged in such a dysfunctional manner that the problem crops up at various times along various fault lines until the underlying system itself is addressed. When we practice systems thinking, what we are doing is exploring the context within our connections with others and with organizations, understanding and respecting the perspectives that each actor within the system brings, and trying to define the scope and scale of what might be needed to begin to make improvements. This kind of thinking enables us to tackle the large-scale problems facing our world today, learning and depending on one another within the institutions that we foster.Systems thinking is crucial to problem-solving, because no problem exists in isolation, all are part of a larger system of interacting networks.

Convergent Thinking

When you break down the term convergent thinking, you come out with two pieces: convergent can mean a variety of ideas coming together to form one specific conclusion. Thought is obviously what we have been talking about throughout this entire book.

When you put the terms together, convergent thinking can be defined as a problem-solving technique that enables a variety of different people from different backgrounds and occupations to come to the best conclusion about a bright, well-understood question. This thinking strategy is used to develop a fast, logical answer to a problem. By using convergent thinking, a group can solve problems at a quicker pace as long as they can agree on a solution. This train of thought can be considered lacking in creativity, but it is efficient.Therefore, while it has cons, it also has pros. This type of thinking is suitable for obtaining straightforward facts, such as the sky is blue, and the Earth is round.

Convergent thinking is used in any standard IQ test. It is also used when there is only one correct answer to a problem. We can say that math problems will utilize a lot of convergent thinking. These tests evaluate things such as pattern recognition, logical flow of thought, and your capacity to solve problems. Multiple-choice questions are also a way to test convergent thinking.

Divergent Thinking

Divergent thinking is defined as a problem-solving strategy which allows a person to see multiple correct answers to a problem and determine which one will work the best. This type of thought process involves creativity and enables you to look at various things at once. You use divergent thinking when you are brainstorming ideas for a paper or freewriting. Through divergence, a person is able to take one approach or statement and branch off to make several different conclusions about that statement. All of these conclusions can be considered correct, and the findings will vary depending on the person.
There are 8 elements of divergent thinking:

1. Complexity: This is your ability to theorize many different ideas that are multilayered.
2. Risk-taking: This is important when considering your ability to set yourself apart from others. Those who venture into the unknown are generally the ones who make new discoveries and find new answers to questions.
3. Elaboration: This is taking one idea and building off of it. For example, Hershey's Chocolate has grown from a simple chocolate bar to several different types of chocolate in various forms which allows for a more enormous amount of productivity.
1. Originality: This is why it is so incredible to see several different people use divergent thinking to come up with an answer to a problem. People will utilize many different trains of thought to come up with new ideas.
2. Imagination: This is important in creating new products and developing new ideas. This also will connect to originality.
3. Flexibility: Your ability to create varied perceptions and categories. This is how we get several variations of the same thing.
4. Curiosity: To create new ideas, you must come up with further questions and inquiries.

1. Fluency: The ability to stimulate many ideas to have many different solutions in case one works better than the other.

People who think divergently share traits such as an inability to conform, persistence, curiosity, and readiness to take risks. There are no personality traits associated with those who engage in convergent thinking. This means that all people engage in convergent thinking. There are no tests to determine divergent thinking.

The two different thinking styles can be compared in several different ways. Studies show that divergent thinking and convergent thinking can affect mood. When prompted to use divergent thinking, a positive atmosphere was triggered, increasing productivity. When prompted to use convergent thinking, a negative attitude was triggered. Different thinkers generally score higher in categories that test word fluency and reading ability.

Divergent thinking is necessary for open-ended problems with even the smallest bit of creativity. Things like sleep deprivation can decrease your ability to think divergently. However, sleep deprivation hardly affects convergent thinking.

Let's look at some examples.

An example of a question that would require convergent thinking would look like this:

Who was the first president of the United States?

1. George Washington

2. Barack Obama
3. Thomas Jefferson
4. Abraham Lincoln

There is only one real answer to this problem – George Washington. This type of problem would not require any critical thinking and is merely
asking for a recitation of your memory.

An example of a question that would require divergent thinking would look like this:

Who was the most influential president of the United States?

There is no one right answer to this question. As long as you were able to gather sufficient evidence, you could choose any president that you wanted. This question requires creativity and would call for originality, as long as you weren't copying off of the person next to you. If you chose a president who maybe did not have a significant impact, you would be taking a risk that could benefit you in the long run as long as you played your cards right.

So how does this all play into critical thinking?

I said before that convergent thinking does not require any critical thought.

This remains true. You would utilize convergent thinking when acquiring information. An excellent example of a convergent thinker is Sherlock Holmes. He used deductive reasoning to solve a slew of crimes. He was able to take in all of the details of a crime scene and make connections to come to one conclusion and answer the question of who committed the crime. This sums up the description and analysis portion of our critical thinking model.

Once you delve into the evaluation portion of our model, you are making the transition to divergent thinking. Divergent thinking would take the answer of who committed the crime and ask more questions about it. For example, once you figure out who committed the crime, you will want to know why the crime was committed, what crimes could be engaged in the future, etc.

Through divergent thinking, we can create profiles and answer questions about future crimes, which lead to more efficient problem-solving. This is where you will begin to see that critical thinking is more of a cycle than a step-by-step process. You can pick up at any point in the critical thinking process and continue onward around and around.

Cognitive Behavioral Therapy

Cognitive Behavioral Therapy CBT)works by emphasizing the relationship between our thoughts, feelings, and behaviors. When you begin to change any of these components, you start to initiate change in the others. The goal of CBT is to help lower the amount of worry you do and increase the overall quality of your life. Here are the 8 basic principles of how Cognitive Behavioral Therapy works:

a.   CBT will help provide a new perspective of understanding your problems.

A lot of times, when an individual has been living with a problem for a long time in their life, they may have developed unique ways of understanding it and dealing with it. Usually, this just maintains the problem or makes it worse. CBT is effective in helping you look at your problem from a new perspective, and this will help you learn other ways of understanding your problem and learning a new way of dealing with it.

a.   CBT will help you generate new skills to work out your problem.

You probably know that understanding a problem is one matter, and dealing with it is entirely another can of worms. To help start changing your problem, you will need to develop new skills that will help you change your thoughts, behaviors, and emotions that are affecting your anxiety and mental health.

For instance, CBT will help you achieve new ideas about your problem and begin to use and test them in your daily life. Therefore, you will be more capable of making up your own mind regarding the root issue that is causing these negative symptoms.

a.   CBT relies on teamwork and collaboration between the client and therapist (or program).

CBT will require you to be actively involved in the entire process, and your thoughts and ideas are extremely valuable right from the beginning of the therapy. You are the expert when it comes to your thoughts and problems.

The therapist is the expert when it comes to acknowledging the emotional issues. By working as a team, you will be able to identify your problems and have your therapist better address them. Historically, the more the therapy advances, the more the client takes the lead in finding techniques to deal with the symptoms.

a.   The goal of CBT is to help the client become their own therapist.

Therapy is expensive; we all know that. One of the goals of CBT is to not have you become overly dependent on your therapist because it is not feasible to have therapy forever. When therapy comes to an end and you do not become your own therapist, you will be at high risk for a relapse.

However, if you are able to become your own therapist, you will be in a good spot to face the hurdles that life throws at you. In addition, it is proven that having confidence in your own ability to face hardship is one of the best predictors of maintaining the valuable information you got from therapy. By playing an active role during your sessions, you will be able to gain the confidence needed to face your problems when the sessions are over.

a.   CBT is succinct and time-limited.

As a rule of thumb, CBT therapy sessions typically last over the course of 10 to 20 sessions. Statistically, when therapy goes on for many months, there is a higher risk of the client becoming dependent on the therapist. Once you have gained a new perspective and understanding of your problem, and are equipped with the right skills, you are able to use them to solve future problems. It is crucial in CBT for you to try out your new skills in the real world. By actually dealing with your own problem hands-on without the security of recurring therapy sessions, you will be able to build confidence in your ability to become your own therapist.

a.   CBT is direction based and structured.

CBT typically relies on a fundamental strategy called 'guided recovery.' By setting up some experiments with your therapist, you will be able to experiment with new ideas to see if they reflect your reality accurately. In other words, your therapist is your guide while you are making discoveries in CBT. The therapist will not tell you whether you are right or wrong but

 instead, they will help develop ideas and experiments to help you test these ideas.

a.   CBT is based on the present, "here and now".

Although we know that our childhood and developmental history play a big role in who we are today, one of the principles of CBT actually distinguishes between what caused the problem and what is maintaining the problem presently. In a lot of cases, the reasons that maintain a problem are different than the ones that originally caused it.

For example, if you fall off while riding a horse, you may become afraid of horses. Your fear will continue to be maintained if you begin to start avoiding all horses and refuse to ride one again. In this example, the fear was called by the fall, but by avoiding your fear, you are continuing to maintain it.

Unfortunately, you cannot change the fact that you had fallen off the horse but you can change your behaviors when it comes to avoidance. CBT primarily focuses on the factors that are maintaining the problem because these factors are susceptible to change.

a. Worksheet exercises are significant elements of CBT therapy.

Unfortunately, reading about CBT or going to one session of therapy a week is not enough to change our ingrained patterns of thinking and behaving.

During CBT, the client is always encouraged to apply their new skills into their daily lives. Although most people find CBT therapy sessions to be very intriguing, it does not lead to change in reality if you do not exercise the skills you have learned.

These eight principles will be your guiding light throughout your Cognitive Behavioral Therapy. By learning, understanding, and applying these eight principles, you will be in a good position to invest your time and energy into becoming your own therapist and achieving your personal goals.

Based on research, individuals who are highly motivated to try exercises outside of sessions tend to find more value in therapy than those who don't. Keep in mind that other external factors still have an effect on your success, but your motivation is one of the most significant factors. By following CBT using the principles above, you should be able to remain highly motivated throughout CBT.

Challenging Your Unhelpful Thinking Styles

Once you are able to identify your own unhelpful thinking styles, you can begin trying to reshape those thoughts into something more realistic and factual. Here, we will be learning how to challenge these thoughts in order to build a healthier thinking style.

Keep in mind that it takes a lot of effort and dedication to change our own thoughts, so don't get frustrated if you are not succeeding right away. You probably have had these thoughts for a while, so don't expect it to change overnight.

Probability Overestimation

If you find that you have thoughts about a possible negative outcome, but you are noticing that you often overestimate the probability, try asking yourself the questions below to re-evaluate your thoughts.

Based on my experience, what is the probability that this thought will come true realistically?

What are the other possible results from this situation? Is the outcome that I am thinking of now the only possible one? Does my feared outcome have the highest probability out of the other outcomes?

Have I ever experienced this type of situation before? If so, what happened? What have I learned from these past experiences that would be helpful to me now?

If a friend or loved one is having these thoughts, what would I say to them?

Catastrophizing

If the prediction that I am afraid of really did come true, how bad would it really be?

If I am feeling embarrassed, how long will this last? How long will other people remember/talk about it? What are all the different things they could be saying? Is it 100% that they will only think bad things?

I am feeling uncomfortable right now, but is this really a horrible or unbearable outcome?

What are the other alternatives for how this situation could turn out?

If a friend or loved one was having these thoughts, what would I say to them?

Mind Reading

Is it possible that I really know what other people's thoughts are? What are the other things they could be thinking about?

Do I have any evidence to support my own assumptions?

In the scenario that my assumption is true, what is so bad about it?

Personalization

What other elements might be playing a role in the situation? Could it be the other person's stress, deadlines, or mood?

Does somebody always have to be at blame?

A conversation is never just one person's responsibility. Were any of these circumstances out of my control?

Should Statements

Would I be holding the same standards to a loved one or a friend?

Are there any exceptions?

Will someone else do this differently?

All or Nothing Thinking

Is there a middle ground or grey area that I am not considering?

Would I judge a friend or loved one in the same way?

Was the entire situation 100% negative? Was there any part of the situation that I handled well?

Is having/showing some anxiety such a horrible thing?

Selective Attention/Memory

What are the positive elements of the situation? Am I ignoring those?

Would a different person see this situation differently? What strengths do I have? Am I ignoring those?

Negative Core Beliefs

Do I have any evidence that supports my negative beliefs? Is this thought true in every situation?

Would a loved one or friend agree with my self-belief?

Once you catch yourself using these unhelpful thinking patterns, ask yourself the above questions to begin changing your own thoughts. Remember, the core basis of CBT is the idea that your own thoughts affect your emotions which then influences your behavior.

LEADERSHIP

Chapter 3:

HOW TO NEGOTIATE

To be a successful negotiator, you must have the right mindset and no type of mindset is more important than staying calm and confident. Most people go into negotiations nervous, anxious, and powerless because they have not studied negotiation techniques. The best way to stay calm and confident in negotiation is by empowering yourself: <u>by acquiring knowledge about negotiation techniques *before* you negotiate, you will walk into the negotiation calm and confident</u>.

Key Technique: Approaching a negotiation nervously or aggressively gives the other party the upper hand. <u>Be calm, civil, and confident</u>. Cutting- edge scientific research shows <u>that this mindset makes you a more effective negotiator</u>. A synthesis of research in the *Harvard Negotiation Law Review* illustrates that a negotiator who is assertive (direct) and empathetic (civil) is the most effective type of negotiator. The study also illustrates negotiators who are stubborn, arrogant, and egotistical are more ineffective negotiators. Further, when an adversarial negotiator is unethical, he is perceived as even less effective.

As you can see, do not feel intimidated, especially by jerks or tyrants.

Bullies can sense weakness and try to take advantage of it. When you learn these negotiation techniques, bullies will no longer bother you. Now lets talk more about staying calm. Studies show that a calm mindset, even in intense situations, leads to better outcomes. You should be careful not to be over-invested emotionally in a negotiation, which causes a loss of perspective, fractured judgment and a focus on bad outcomes. When you are not calm, your negotiations will suffer.

Now we will get a bit more technical and talk about how to make an offer in a negotiation. There have been thousands of studies on this and the research has shown that in your initial offer you should <u>aim high</u> and ask for what you want.

Unfortunately, people mess this one up all the time and their outcomes suffer. Here's how it works.

This concept is called <u>anchoring</u>. Study after study shows that we are <u>unduly influenced by the initial figure</u> we encounter when estimating the value of an item. Anchoring is an attempt to establish a reference point (anchor) around which the negotiation will revolve and a reference point to make negotiation adjustments. <u>Anchoring subconsciously biases one's</u> <u>expectations around the initial number.</u>

Anchoring works great if you make the first offer in a negotiation, but what if you are the one that gets "anchored"? So for example, if your counterpart asks for $200 (anchor) for something you are willing to pay $100 for, you should not respond until you do what *Harvard Law Schools Program on Negotiation* calls "defusing the anchor." In this scenario, before responding to your counterparts $200 offer, you should <u>"defuse" the anchor</u> by making clear that their offer is far from your expectation and not an acceptable one. Harvard suggests saying something along the lines of, "I'm not trying to play games with you, but we are miles apart on price."

Harvard notes that an all too often mistake is to respond to an unacceptable offer with a counteroffer before defusing the anchor. In the above example, if you don't defuse the offer, you are implying that your counterparty's $200 offer is within the realm of possibility and it will be used as the anchor.

After you defuse the anchor, you can then make a counteroffer which is much more in line with your expectations (but remember, don't offer what you are willing to settle for. Aim for something better. The principle discussed right before this still applies). So in our example, you could say something like: "I am not trying to play games with you, but we are very far apart on price. I am willing to offer $75."

Anchoring is a proven concept in study after study in all types of negotiations so this concept is going to apply in most of your negotiations. In a number of studies, "researchers have shown that opening offers and demands, insurance policy caps, statutory damage caps, negotiator aspirations, and other "first numbers" can influence negotiation outcomes in transactions and settlements."

So make sure to use anchoring if you are making the initial offer and to "defuse" your counterparty's anchor if they make the initial offer and it is far off from what you are looking for.

Tip: Studies show how powerful anchoring is, even in extreme examples. One research study asked participants how old Gandhi was when he died, framing the question for the first group as "before or after age 9," and framing the question for the second group as "before or after age 140." The anchoring affect was powerful: the first group guessed 50 on average, and the second grouping guessed 67 on average.

When most people think of negotiation, they are understandably focused on themselves and their needs. But the key to a successful negotiation is to focus on your counterpart as well: to actively listen and understand what their priorities are. This active listening shows empathy (ability to understand your counterpart's emotions) and builds trust.

Scientific research consistently shows how active listening leads to better negotiation outcomes. For example, research consistently shows that the more salespeople talk, the less they tend to close sales, and the more salespeople let the customer talk, the more sales they win.

So it is extremely important to listen to your counterpart in a negotiation.

When you listen, people will tell you what they want and what they are feeling. This is key because <u>you have to understand what the other side</u> <u>wants in order to have a successful negotiation</u>.

A win-win negotiation does not mean you need to compromise and give up what you <u>truly</u> want. Instead, a win-win is where the <u>agreement you reach</u> with your <u>counterpart cannot be improved by further discussions</u>. In sum, your outcome cannot be improved for your benefit and the agreement for the other side cannot be improved further for their benefit, either.

If you are able to negotiate a win-win, it leads to <u>long term benefits in the</u> <u>relationship</u> between you and the other party. For example, if you are negotiating with a company, a win-win can lead to a positive long-term relationship with that company. A *Harvard* study makes an important observation: If something is important to you, absolutely negotiate. But don't argue over every little detail. If you fight in order to get just a little bit more, it may rub your counterpart the wrong way. This can limit your ability to negotiate with the company later in your career.

Example: It is the end of the month and you are looking to buy a new car. You want to pay 12K for the car while the salesman is asking for 15K. By actively listening and understanding his motivations (Chapter 4), you learn that the salesman needs to meet his sales quota of selling 15 cars by the end of the month in 2 days. If he meets his quota, he will get a large bonus from his employer. You tell the salesman that if he meets your price of 12K (your win), he will be much more likely to meet his quota and get his bonus (his win). So, while the car salesman will get less commission on your individual purchase, it is a win-win because your purchase will help the car salesman to meet his quota and get his bonus.

Example: These techniques also work well in personal conflicts. For example, in a negotiation to solve a financial dispute with a friend, people often have different priorities and a win-win is possible. *Harvard* gives a good example here. Some parties may place a higher value on receiving a formal apology whereas others may be more concerned about the money. If Party A places a high value on receiving a formal apology and Party B places a high value on the financial aspect of the dispute, Party B may be willing to apologize to Party A in exchange for owing Party A less money.

Win-win negotiation is especially important when you plan to have an ongoing relationship with the other party. You may be negotiating with a company that you plan to work at for a long time or you may want to buy another car from the same dealer. In a personal conflict, you certainly will want to have an ongoing relationship with a spouse or close friend (hopefully).

But I do live in the real world and I know that sometimes your counterparty may be a jerk and not focused on a win-win. What do you do in these situations? You use the strategies in this book! They even work when dealing with people you do not like. As I discussed before, you need to separate the person from the problem. Even the biggest jerks out there have the human need to be heard so you come into the negotiation with the right mindset and stay calm (Chapter 1), prepare beforehand (Chapter 2), use anchoring (chapter 3), and actively listen (Chapter 4). And lastly, you use the next two techniques in this book. In the next chapter (Chapter 6), I will discuss the importance of using creative options and how this can lead to a desirable outcome. And, in the very worst-case scenario when dealing with jerks and tyrants, you walk away (which I will discuss in Chapter 7). No negotiation is worth you being abused and/or taken advantage of.

Another important aspect of negotiating with difficult people is not to get overly emotional and sway away from a "win-win" mentality. To illustrate how powerful the concepts in this book are, studies show that when people get overly emotionally invested in a negotiation with an unlikeable counterpart, it could lead to a <u>lose-lose</u> negotiation outcome. Think about that: <u>People are willing to even hurt their own interests so they can "hurt" an unlikeable opponent</u>. Do not do this! Stay calm and focused and separate the person from the problem. If you are flustered, walk away.

The Importance of Your "BATNA" (Best Alternative to a Negotiated Agreement)

The ability to walk away is arguably the most important negotiation technique. You may have noticed that the best negotiators have the least to lose if a negotiation does not work out. Much more often than not, the most successful negotiation party will be the one who can walk away from the negotiation without experiencing a significant loss. <u>You gain leverage when you are *truly* willing to walk away from a negotiation if the proposed outcome does not meet your needs</u>.

But isn't this just all luck, you say? Don't some people inherently have better options? Not at all. The very best negotiators plan ahead so that they can walk away if they need to. They do this by <u>creating options beforehand</u>. Previously, we talked about the power of creating options during a negotiation. This part will deal with creating alternative options if the negotiation itself does not work out (we are leaving no stone unturned in this book!).

In the book *Getting to Yes*, the authors introduced an idea that can help us best understand this concept: the "best alternative to a negotiated agreement" (BATNA). Alternative to a negotiated agreement is what you would do on your own if you cannot reach an agreement. The best of these choices is your BATNA.

Before you enter your negotiation, you should already have planned your BATNA and get creative about developing a better one if your initial BATNA is not good enough. <u>The better your BATNA is, the easier it will be</u> <u>for you to walk away</u>. Lets look at a couple examples of BATNA.

Example:
You are negotiating with Cindy to buy her car. Cindy asks you for 15K to buy her car. *Before* you go to the negotiating table with Cindy, you should research what alternatives are available to you if you do not buy Cindy's car. Let's say that you find a similar car is available at a dealer for 12K. Therefore, your BATNA is buying the car from the dealer for 12K. So you will use the negotiating techniques identified in this book and then, if Cindy is not willing to sell the car for 12K or below, you will walk away from the deal. <u>*Walk away when your BATNA is better than your counterpart's final*</u> <u>*offer.*</u>

Example:
Researchers have also identified many examples of potential BATNAs, some most people don't often consider.

Walking away from the entire deal.
Going to an alternative supplier/dealer/seller. Buying a different product or service.
Delaying the negotiation or deal.
Changing the specifications or components of a deal. Changing the person you are negotiating with.

Maintaining the status quo and keeping the current arrangements. Negotiating with another part of the organization or going above the person with whom you are negotiating.

As you can see, there are many examples of the broad ways you can determine your BATNA. Think creatively about your BATNA before you go into your negotiation.

The *Harvard Law School Program on Negotiation* has provided further excellent research on BATNA in very recent years. Results of their studies have revealed the following:

Do not reveal a weak BATNA - When you need to make a deal with a counterparty no matter what, your counterparty will sense your weakness and take advantage. Never go into a negotiation without considering your BATNA and trying to make it stronger beforehand.

Bluffing - As in poker, some parties may bluff and threaten to walk away (even if they don't have a good BATNA). I do not recommend this strategy. Not only are the ethical implications questionable, but this is a very high-risk strategy because it will only (maybe) work if your counterparty does not have a good BATNA either.

Do Not Reveal your BATNA too early – if you reveal your BATNA it could come across as a threat to the other party (and damage the "trust" principle as discussed in Chapter 4).

Work to Actively Improve Your BATNA – If your BATNA is not good enough, figure out ways to improve it before you enter the negotiation.

Tip: Earlier in this book, we talked about negotiating with jerks. If someone is transparently trying to get their way with no concessions to you or is not negotiating in good faith, walk away! Remember, negotiation should be ethical and a give and take between the two parties. There is no reason you need to be taken advantage of. Just walk away.

Chapter 4:

HOW TO FACE A FAILURE

Only a few folks make fun out of a fall. Far too great a number of us rather see it as a disaster. We dread to nosedive, we dread a fall, we dread a failure. The reasons are not far – fetched. People either make you a laughing stalk, intentionally walk away from you, or more painfully refuse to offer a helping hand when you fall. Those who have fallen before can tell the story better.

The fallen is either viewed as a fool, an imperfect person or a novice. I have observed that what is tragic about falling is the attitude of those around us most especially those we really expect to encourage that state. For mature minds, this attitude may somewhere be strengthening because it is not new after all. But for weak minds, it could be deadly and devastating because not many people have the capacity to cope with the rejection which follows a failure.

You can't make a fun until you've learnt the necessary lessons God intents for you in the experience, until you've put it in the right light, until you've put the experience behind. Putting failure in the right is the greatest challenge of most of us. A vast majority of us often resign to fate after a failing experience and refuse to explore the possibility of life after a fall, the possibility of future success.

In bringing out the best in people, Alan Loy McGinnis creatively penned down some words regarding the management of failure. he says, the different ways in which different people react to failure is a motivational puzzle. What is that causes some to sail forth into the world with great promise and a strong trajectory, then quit after only one defeat?

Unable to rise from their failure, they scale down their dreams and live out their lives in resignation and cautious mediocrity. On the other hand, what causes some to be capable of endless renewal? Failure seems only to make them more determined to overcome, and when they stumble, they pick themselves up, look around to learn from their mistakes and then go on to finish the race with distinction.

Those who have been able to make their fall fun are those who have intentionally overcome the hurt of their supposed failure. We can only make fun out of what gives us please, out of what we find enjoyable. But for everything that gives us or reminds us of pains, we would traditionally dread. Only those who have overcome the fear of failure find it as fun.

The best parameter with which to judge the way you relate to your failure is the way you feel each time you talk about it. Any failing experience you are always scared to talk about, it is an indication that you are yet to overcome its negative effect on you; it is an indication that it is still having a field day on you!

No one is without a failure. The only difference is that some of us quickly put them far behind us and keep reinventing ourselves, keep forging ahead, ahead, and ensure we right our wrong every now and then. We often miss it before we eventually fix it.

No one ever becomes great without failures. It seems that greatness goes along the highway of failures. Hardly can you find a celebrated achiever who will not make reference to failures, unless egocentric and dishonest folks. But how are they able to achieve so much without sinking in the ocean of their mistakes.

Richard J. Needham seems to have the answer: "Strong people make as many and ghastly mistakes as weak people. The difference is that strong people admit them, laugh at them, and learn from them. That is how they become strong".

The analogy that best explains the enthusiasm of falling is that of a child who is learning to walk. The little baby stumble a couple of times, but that never deters him from further attempts. He stands up time and again, cries when necessary and keeps moving. The toddler stumbles enthusiastically because his to walk has come.

No amount of injury and pain dare keep him down from crawling and walking. The fun of learning to walk supersedes the unavoidable pangs of stumbling. To him, stumbling feels so good. The agony of his repeated falls produces a sense of steady growth in him, because falling is a natural process of learning to walk well.

In the same vein, whenever we stumble in the face of any adventure, we should never think of it as a strange phenomenon or take the thought of quitting but to rather stay on the track of success and keep up our dreams. Hence we foresee success at the end, little stumbling here and there shouldn't deter us from staying on till we breast the tape of success.

To stumble means you are making progress. Because no one stumbles sitting down. You only stumble when moving. It was American's twenty sixth presidents, Theodore Roosevelt who once said, "The only man who never makes a mistake is the man who never does anything".

In his message Failure is Not Fatal, Denny Curran the senior pastor of River of Life Church, Cold Spring, Minnesota frankly said, "If you don't fall it means you are not trying. If you never failed chances are that you never tried anything". He rather discouraged us from letting failure settle right inside of us as well as killing the thought of quitting in the face of any failure.

"When failure gets inside of you it will force you to give up, to quit. Failure does not make you a failure, quitting does, "he further said: the essence of falling or failure is to learn how to do it better and not to stop trying. Because as a rule:

He who never falls never stands firm

He who never fights never wins

He who never fails never succeeds

He who never stumbles is never humble

He who never groans never grows

He who is never laughed at never laughs

He who is never mocked never makes sense

He who is never fired is never fired up

And he who is never battered is never better.

Some of us only get to do things better after we've first messed things up, after we've gotten it all wrong all the way. To me, it is normal to mess things up most especially when we are learning to do them for the first time. But it may not be totally acceptable to run through life messing up.

Falling exempts no one. Both sinners and saints stumble. The only difference is where each party turns after the experience, where they seek their solutions, and what the experience makes out of them. Except a novice, every righteous person ought to know that life plays it out evenly.

Everyone gets his or her chunk in life. No amount of prayers can prevent life's hurt on the believer. As a matter of fact, God would be unfair to the rest of the world to exempt Christians from suffering. He would also be producing weaklings for children if He makes life too comfortable for us.

He allows us to go through life's hurts in order for us to develop the capacity to handle life's issues by ourselves. Our numerous falling fortify us to face life squarely. David, a man of a wealth of experience when it comes to life matter said, "For a righteous may fall seven times and rise again". I wrote in one of my books "Falling is not as important as rising and moving on".

I feel our attitude should not be to resent our failure but to rather fail forward, to rather fail productively.

In Where Is God When It Hurts? Philip Yancey also wrote an illustration similar to my analogy of a boy who is learning to walk. He used the illustration to drive home the importance of stumbling as well as suffering in the life of the believer or even anybody living on the planet earth. I feel his thought equally makes some pretty sense:

To help understand, think of an illustration from a human family. A father determined to exclude all pain from his beloved daughter's life would never allow her to take a step. She might fall down! Instead, he picks her up and carries her wherever she goes or pushes her in a carriage.

Over time such a pampered child will become an individual, unable to take a step, totally dependent on her father.

Such a father, no matter how loving would end up failing in his most important task: to nurture an independent person into adulthood. It would be far better for the daughter herself if her father stands back and lets her walk, even if it means allowing her to stumble.

One of the most unforgettable experiences of my life lived with me from birth till I was 15. Bedwetting, for most children, end in their cradle. But I actually stopped bedwetting at the age of 15 while in form 4 in secondary school. I was severally embarrassed by my parents and foster parents respectively whenever I wet the bed.

At times, my foster parent (my grandmother) would parade me around the village alongside some family members displaying my urine – soaked mat before the villagers as well as passerby. The most painful aspect of it was that, I would be paraded in the morning hour before my school mates from neighboring villages (who were schooling in our village).That continued till I was fifteen as a secondary school boy. To them, the entire idea was to embarrass me till I would stop the act. But unfortunate, none of those techniques was a success.

I remember I was always ashamed of myself in school. Some of my school mates who lived in the same village with me did not even help matter. They also spread the news in school, and I was mocked by so many. I actually did everything possible to stop bedwetting, but it was to no avail.

The experience naturally ended the very night I gave my life to Christ twenty fives ago. Jesus did not only save me from my sins, He equally delivered me from that shameful experience.

Guess what? I now freely talk about it everywhere and even laugh at myself when talking about it. The reason is because it's no longer a painful experience for me. One, it's been put far behind me. Two, it's no longer a current occurrence in my life. any experience you find difficult to laugh at might still be having some painful effect on you, and you may never learn any lesson from it. Those who laugh at themselves hardly take the mockery of others personal. Laughing at yourself is a creative way of feeling good – stumbling, feeling cool failing.

Failure usually wears a destructive façade at the inception and makes us feel as if we have come to our wits' end. This also contributes to why many a people quickly see their failure as a dead end instead of an end to an old life and the beginning of a new experience. Not many see failure as a process. Most of us see it as final. And it is our perspective that usually determines the impact failure would have on us.

Each time you see failure as finality, it prevents you from facing life with passion and courage. But when you see it as a mere process or a product of one phase of your invention, you quickly summon up the courage to reinvent yourself and keep forging ahead.

The truth is, failure happens! But the question is what happens after every failure? What do you deduce from it? He does it eventually leave you? Failure can either make you groan or make you grow. It can equally create both effects on you. It either fortifies you or leaves you frustrated.

Dr. Tournier admits that suffering may push a person towards brokenness and not toward personal growth. It will always have the former effect on anyone who never sees it as a transforming agent. But everyone who sees failure or suffering as an agent of transformation gets easily transformed after any such hurting experiences.

I have personally being through all kind of seasons you can think of. I am acquainted with hunger and starvation too well. I have faced with hatred and rejection right from childhood into any adult life. Poverty and pains were just regular visitors. I have known suffering and insufficiency a couple of times. I have failed numerously, yet none of those experiences has ever left me worse than it ever met me.

They've always left me better off, they've always equipped me with enough capability to face and of course conquer whatever comes my way hereafter.

Never let a failure leave you damaged but rather developed. When David had a moral failure by sleeping with Uriah's wife, he initially tried to sweep it under the carpet. But when God made the gravity of his offense clear to him, he immediately repented of his error, made necessary adjustments and requested a clean heart, a renewed spirit, God's constant presence and the restoration of the joy of salvation.

Uriah's wife's experience left David broken and equally led to a personal growth in his moral life. Although he still had many wives, but he never got any one of them through the same way he got Bathsheba.

Where I have become a kinder person due to numerous bitter experiences in my life, there are equally known folks who have rather become more cruel and revengeful. Response or reaction is a function of the individual's level of understanding and growth. They both have their functional effects.

Those who react to situations rarely learn any lesson from them, hardly grow beyond their present state of life. But those who respond to challenges change the course of their lives at will, become better mentors, and before long turn their setbacks into a starling success story.

Naturally, we often face negative event with a reactionary attitude. We are always quick to ask the wrong questions like – why did this happen to me. Do I deserve this after all? Why not someone else? You don't get a good response each time you react. But every time you respond, you ask the right questions such as, what did I do wrong to warrant this?

What was I supposed to have done to bring about a reverse experience? What lesson do I deduce from this? What message is God really passing across to me? As a rule, each time you respond like this, you get the situation fixed and you move to the nest level of your life.

Writing under the chapter God Helps Those Who Stop Hurting Themselves, Rabbi Kushner said, "Too often, in our pain and confusion, we instinctively do the wrong thing. We don't feel we deserve to be helped, so we let guilt, anger, jealousy, and self – imposed loneliness make a bad situation even worse".

But when we learn the appropriate lessons and make our lives better despite the unpleasant experience that to me is one of the benefits of failure and adversity.

Harold Kushner also observed the difference people's lives would have when they handle their unwanted situation responsively. He says, "When people who were never particularly strong become strong in the face of adversity, when people who tended to think only of themselves become unselfish and heroic in an emergency.

I have to ask myself where they got these qualities which they would freely admit they did not have before. My answer is that this is one of the ways in which God helps us when we suffer beyond the limits of our own strength".

The strongest point of great men and women universally is the courage to pick up their piece and move on no matter the wreck or failure. They may bemoan their pains but they never bury their heads in them. They always quickly brace up and re – launch their prior ideas or new ones. This attitude never makes to bow out of life as failures. You can't go any far in life if you look too frequently behind you, if you lament your mess beyond necessary measure.

One of my New Testament heroes is Apostle Paul

who was describe by an author whose book I read several years ago as the second greatest man who had ever lived after Christ. He didn't earn this praise because he attended the best Theological seminary of his time, neither did he qualify for this because of his foremost profession as a lawyer.

Or perhaps he became the great apostle that he was because of his social connection as a member of the Sanhedrin or a Pharisee in the Jewish religion. All of these were mere foundations upon which he built his latter life.

What really qualified Apostle Paul the position of being the second greatest man after Jesus Christ were his many trials, suffering, failures, setbacks, shipwrecks and infirmities – a replica of Jesus' history. Isaiah the prophet prophetically described Jesus as "A man of sorrows and acquainted with grief...." The writer of the book of Hebrews summarized what gave Jesus the prime place in human history.

He writes, "For it was fitting for Him, for whom are all things and by whom are all things, in bringing many sons to glory, to make the captain of their salvation perfect through suffering".

Paul was not the only apostle who suffered many things. Virtually all the pioneering apostle did suffer a great deal. Some of them were beheaded, some were flayed to death, some were crucified head downward, and some shot to death by a shower of arrows, amongst others. But what made Paul's case quite different was that he suffered far above every one of them and yet he wouldn't give up the course of the cross.

After every suffering and pain, he would always pick up his pieces and move on to break the hard land with the gospel of Christ. He suffered joyfully and endured pains passionately. Hear how he summarized his glory experiences:

...Are they ministers of Christ? – I speak as a fool I am more in labours more abundant, in stripes above measure, in prisons more frequently, in deaths often. From the Jews five times I received forty stripes minus one. Three times I was beaten with rods, once I was stoned; three times I was shipwrecked, a night and a day I have been in the deep.

In journeys often, in perils of the Gentiles, in perils in the city, in perils in the wilderness, in perils in the sea, in perils among false brethren, in weariness and toil, in sleeplessness often, in hunger and thirst, in fasting often, in cold and nakedness...." To mention just a few.

One may ask, "How was he able to achieve so much in the face of all those historical facts. Paul never got stuck in any situation for too long. However killing the case may be, Paul had a ready – made answer to them all" none of these move me, nor do I count my life dear to myself, so that I may finish my race with joy...."

Since our modern age now propagates human rights virtually in every aspect of life – right to live, right to marry whoever or whatever sex feels good to you, right to information technology, right to vote and be voted for, right of expression etc. I also feel that everyone should be allowed the right to fail and fix their lives afterwards without being condemned, without being rejected and without being viewed as fools.

When people have a sense of human right to failure without a labeling, it would be far easier for everyone to brace up, pick up their pieces and move on most especially when the word around them makes it enabling.

To forge ahead in the face of failure requires real courage because you will always be left alone to mourn your misery, perhaps to die in that condition or to see bailing yourself out. Obviously, you are to fix your life after any failure – no one else does that for you.

Don't blow your failure out of proportion; there is nothing strange anywhere to anyone. Millions of people are simultaneously facing whatever you are facing; the only problem is that you are not seeing beyond your immediate environment, beyond the side of the mountain you are facing. And that has made you to make a mountain out of your molehill. In Never Say Never, Phyllis George shows us how she handled her difficult situations through the support of her friends and family members, as well as giving time a pretty chance to heal up her wounds and by giving every situation the right interpretation.

Distance and time are very important in getting over a difficult situation. I had tried and failed, but in the end I learned to be kind to myself. I may have failed at the job, but I wasn't a failure, she said. No matter the amount of failures or setbacks we may be experiencing now, it is a matter of time they will become history provided we don't allow them to swallow us up.

Robert H. Schuller advises, "It is amazing what God can do if we will give Him a little time to work His plan out".

Chapter 5:

HOW TO MANAGE TIME

In this chapter, you will learn the best techniques we have tried for managing time when you have a lot of busy schedules. Let's make a summary immediately and then analyze them specifically:

You don't manage time, you manage yourself

Define priorities

Divide by step

Finding a "Place of Productivity"

Use downtime

The "boxes" of time

Use weekends (in moderation)

I'm in the office and I'm answering the last email of the day, because then I'll have to get ready to go to the station, take the train and go home to prepare for a university exam that I'll have in just over a month. Until this summer, I would never have imagined leaving home at 7 am, returning at 7 pm and sitting on a desk to study. I have always organized everything in order to finish my things to do at 5 pm, and then dedicate myself to the most total fooling around until 11 pm. But now I work, study, and also try to have a fairly peaceful social life. If I hadn't learned to better manage my time, I would have given up everything after a week of work. I learned how it feels in these cases: in the morning at the university, in the afternoon I study, physical activity, coffee with friends, but the day seems not to be enough. Let alone if you add a job, where is the time to "live"?

Small premise: what I am about to illustrate, as I have already told you, are 7 time management techniques that I have personally tried and that allow me to do all my duties during the day. (I'm honest, sometimes it happens that I can't do everything, but it happens to anyone, whoever writes the opposite doesn't just say it because otherwise they are no longer an expert in the sector) However, what I am about to share would not work if there was not a minimum of sacrifice and a lot of determination to reach a goal. If you are not part of that group of human beings who in life want to fight to pursue their dream, stop reading my words. If, on the other hand, you are part of the remaining 1%, let's get serious.

YOU DON'T MANAGE TIME, YOU MANAGE YOURSELF

I'll be short and concise. The day we have available every day consists of 24 hours. Of these 24 hours, on average 6/7 (at least hopefully) we spend them rightfully sleeping. Therefore 17/18 hours remain.

No technique, no application will increase them or stop time.

We will always have that number of hours available. Therefore it is wrong to think: "I must have more time". Instead, let's think about "managing time better". It seems trivial, but like all trivial things it is often forgotten. From personal experience, I tell you that trying to always stay at night, sleep fewer hours to close yourself off to study or do anything else is useless. It means not having used the hours we had before. Right now you are thinking: "But if I am at university in the morning and I have to study in the afternoon, what hours should I use in your genius?"

You are not completely wrong, but I can assure you that the time we have available during university (if we really want to quantify it) we will never have it again in our entire life. Work, a house to manage if you go to live alone, are all commitments that are added to those you already have and often take up double the hours compared to the University if we do not know how to organize them. Our duty today should technically only be that of students (or so we have been taught).

Unfortunately, life is not like that for everyone, but basically once we have studied it we shouldn't have other urgent obligations to carry on. The gym, friends, competitive sport... are all activities that we could manage independently. How do you do it in the best way? With the second technique of this article. Keep this in mind because it's the most important of all: setting priorities.

Let's see how it works together.

DEFINE PRIORITIES

Many times in high school I used to make it to the end of the day and say "today I did a lot of things, I'm very tired". At the same time I realized that there were still many pages to study and it was already dinner time. It will have happened to all of you to find yourself in such a situation. Analyzing it today, I realized that I actually did a lot of things during the day (gym, study, kept up to date on marketing blogs, watched TV series, helped my parents with some errands, etc.) but I did them in the wrong order. So, taking stock of the day just passed, my most important goal, that is to prepare myself for the question I had to do, had not been completed. Instead of taking even an hour to seriously study, I did it for 20 minutes, then I was distracted by a message from my friend who had a problem and wanted to talk about it, it was time to run errands, finished those errands I went to the gym and in the evening I went home.

None of this would have happened if I had prepared things to do based on priorities. Defining priorities means understanding which are the objectives to be achieved absolutely during the day, which can be started and even not finished, which are not important and can shift to the next day. Only in this way can you be sure not to forget the important things to do and carry them out.

I'll give you an example that can also be applied to the activities we propose to do on the platform. Let's say that tomorrow you have an exam, this afternoon you are free and you just have to accompany your mother to do the shopping. In addition, there is a personal project on start2impact that you want to complete to acquire points and grow your radar skill. Immediately after lunch, it's time to prioritize afternoon activities and get to work.

You could proceed like this:

1st STEP: *review for the exam (it has a mandatory deadline).*

At least for an hour from 3 to 4 pm your concentration must be only on this goal. No Instagram stories to check, no friends to console. For that period of time your focus will be solely and exclusively on books or on repetition of key topics. In this way you should be able to go through the exam decently without having to open the books again until tomorrow. (If you have prepared properly, a requirement that I take for granted)

2nd STEP: *project for start2impact (it is important for your future)*

Once you have finished studying, your brain will

surely tell you that you will have time tomorrow to think about the project of the start2impact Super Guide, now you could do something more relaxing. This is another way to never carry out that project, and not to become part of the 1% of young people in Italy who anticipate their entry into the labor market by 5 years compared to their peers. Roll up your hands, and by dedicating even just an hour to your work, you could easily achieve an excellent result.

3 ° STEP: *expense (it is a necessity, but you could also do it tomorrow)*

If you finished studying at 4pm, took a little break and worked on your project, you might have half an hour to get ready and go shopping that your mother reminds you of since you were around the house when you woke up and looking for caffeine. What not to do: in that period of time between the end of the project and the expense, absolutely avoid watching an episode of your TV series or wasting time on Instagram. You would end up getting lost in the famous phrase "the last episode and then I'll go", from which you never leave. Anyway, after shopping, you should be able to get home around 7pm. Before dinner you would still have time to review or do other activities, but I would say that you may already be satisfied. In this way you will have completed all the goals of the day, you will not find yourself having to revise at night, and indeed you can even enjoy a good movie on the sofa before going to sleep.

Obviously, this was a made-up situation, which I only used to make you understand that if you focus 100% first on the most important things, until you climb to those that you can even postpone, you can accomplish all our goals.

There is one thing I have not told you to ensure that the priority system works properly, and it is contained in the next council.

DON'T THINK ABOUT THE TOTAL THINGS TO DO, DIVIDE THE ACTIVITIES IN STEPS

If only I thought every morning about all the things to do during the day, the only answer my brain would give me is: "stay in bed, it's better". Raise your hand who at least once in their life has experienced that weight between the throat and the stomach (they call it "anxiety") that takes us when we think of the myriad of things to do that await us. In 90% of cases, the anxiety is so strong that we react by doing nothing of what we had set for ourselves. The night before we were so energized and determined to do everything.

After only 6 hours our attitude changed.

All this is normal, because our brains generally tend to see things as a whole, and not to unpack them in single steps, which is much more difficult on a cognitive level. Instead, we should train ourselves to divide the activities to be carried out into many small blocks and distribute them throughout the day, dividing them by priority. The tool that helps me the most in this case is my Mac's simple and innocent calendar. Exactly.

For many years it has been there in silence, never used. Today he became my best friend. Every morning I take ten minutes to organize the things I have to do throughout the day, I calculate on average how much time I need to do them and arrange them in blocks on the calendar. There is only one rule to follow, and I have already explained it to you: first the activities with high priority, then medium, finally low. If unfortunately, as often happens, I see that not everything goes into the day, I move the low priority activities to the next day or even to the week after if they are really unimportant. Many times it happened to me in the morning to have in mind a dozen things to do during the day. When I went to arrange them on the calendar, on the other hand, I understood that the fundamental ones to do were perhaps 6, and the other 4 I could distribute during the week, considerably lightening the workload.

This technique takes 10 minutes a day, but it also saves me several hours sometimes.

FIND YOUR "PLACE OF PRODUCTIVITY"

This is a super effective technique especially when it comes to studying. While there is no real ideal place to study or work, I definitely recommend trying many different ones and finding what I call a "Place of Productivity". That is, a physical space in which we can concentrate to the maximum and do something productively without wasting time. Some like to shut up in their own room, others even can't stand silence and prefer crowded public places like parks, or quieter but with some background noise such as libraries. The trick of this technique does not lie in which place you choose to use, but it consists in associating that place with work or study inside your head. For example, my place of productivity is the dining room table in my home. In particular, I always sit on the chair that is placed in front of the wall and the window. This is extremely useful to me because I know that when I sit there, it really works.

I have no other distractions, and I don't even look for them because my brain automatically knows that this is my place of productivity, and it is used to work. If I want to waste time, there is the sofa next to it.

This too seems trivial. But I assure you that if this automatism is triggered every time you are in your favorite place to study / work, it will be very easy to save time and be more productive.

USE THE DOWNTIME

How many times do we get stuck in traffic for hours, or on a train, on the subway, in line at the post office. During the day we have a lot of dead times, often very long. Most of the time we fill them up by checking the Facebook or Instagram feed. How much time could we gain instead if we used the downtime productively?

What I often do, if I am late with the study for

example, is to hear the recordings of the lesson on the train, so when I come home to study I already know what was talked about in class and I don't have to waste an hour before writing notes or studying on the book.

Or, if I want to know the latest Digital Marketing news, but I'm in the car, instead of reading blog posts, I listen to podcasts from industry experts without having to distract myself from driving.

Downtime, when not very short, is a great resource for gaining precious minutes and doing something of value for our personal growth.

I'm not saying that you have to study in this period of time or do something demanding, that is done in places of productivity. They are simply useful for fixing some concepts in mind or for doing chores that take less time, but that save us the work that we should do later.

THE "BOXES OF TIME"

This is one of the techniques most used by the Project Managers of many large companies.

(In short, the Project Manager is the one who plans the realization of a project or a business activity taking into account costs, resources, purpose and quality).

However, this does not mean that time boxes cannot be used even by a "simple" student.

How do they work?

Essentially, the rule they rely on is one: set a strict deadline, and consider your goal achieved only if the deadline is met.

Said like this it means saying everything and saying nothing.

Let's see how they apply to the study for example.

It will have happened to everyone, as I said in point 3, to be frightened by the amount of time needed to carry out an activity such as studying, and to postpone it indefinitely.

This happens because in our heads we often don't have in mind how much time to devote to that activity, so we perceive it as infinite.

Personally, when it happens to me, I decide to dedicate a "box" of time to her, even short (eg 30 minutes), but intense.

I know that after those 30 minutes of serious work I can go back to doing something that relaxes me more.

In this way, I not only save time because I spent 30 minutes on an important activity and I won't have to study those things in the next study session, but I also beat another arch enemy of our generation:

Procrastination.

If I had listened to my mind, I would never have started studying those pages because I was too scared of sitting for who knows how long in a chair.

In this way instead, not only have I started, but often I feel so satisfied with my willpower that I extend the time box by another 10 minutes, adding

another paragraph to what I have already studied.

In short, where is it written that every activity must necessarily last an indefinite number of hours?

USE WEEKENDS (WITH MODERATION)

Don't take me for a fool. I'm the first to sanctify the weekend and use it to have a great time. We are young, if we don't do it now when should we do it? That said, I am also of the opinion that some moments of the weekend can be used to lighten the workload of the following week, or to finish something that we have left aside during the week itself. Let's go to the meat, as we like at start2impact. Friday evening, sacrosanct outing with friends. Someone returns early, someone else a little later. My advice is to use Saturday mornings to rest your mind and body as they say. If you want to sleep a few hours longer than expected, do it without problems. You can do other activities in the afternoon. And if you don't have time in the afternoon, are you telling me? Simple, wake up a little earlier, but still later than your weekly routine. You can carry out your commitments in the morning and relax in the afternoon. As far as I'm concerned, I find it essential to sleep even one more hour on the weekend, because it seems as if my body and mind perceive a week of rest instead of just one hour. Obviously there are people who need less sleep, perhaps their outlet is another. The important thing is to find it to make you feel 10 times more relaxed and free from any tension. That said, unless you are a robot, it is normal that sooner or later there will come that feeling of anxiety and guilt due to the fact that you have rested. You know that weight that seems to say "You have to do something, you have to do something"? Exactly that.

To solve this problem, I usually use (both on Saturdays and Sundays) the hours immediately following lunch.

Instead of sleeping or sinking my body shape on the sofa as many people do, I arrive already rested and can study, or I can finish some unfinished business. As you can see, there is no need to sacrifice the whole weekend. If the work during the week was done well, sometimes there is no need to use it. But if we are overwhelmed with commitments, despite the large organization, we can allow ourselves a few hours to align with everything, and dedicate the rest of the time to ourselves.

Chapter 6:

HOW TO INVEST MONEY

You probably are thinking that you've won most of the battle when it comes to personal financial management the moment you've learned to save. I can't say I blame you for thinking along these lines because most people can't even get around to saving. They're always looking at their expenses. They're always looking at their long-term liabilities and they never really get around to saving much of anything.

If anything, savings happens at the end of the budget process. They would get their income, and then they would immediately take out their expenses and their liabilities and whatever is left over maybe goes to savings, assuming it survives luxury expenses or entertainment expenses. It is no surprise that given this situation, most Americans don't even have $2,000 in the bank.

As I've mentioned in the introduction, if they were forced by circumstances to cut a check for $2,000, almost half of American households cannot cut that check. They know it's going to bounce. They know they're going to get into trouble if they issue that check. That's how bad things are on a household to household basis, as far as American personal financial management goes.

Since you are able to save, you have overcome that. You have developed a very powerful discipline that enables you to pay yourself first. A lot of people budget their income in a way where savings comes last. You and other savers, on the other hand, think differently. You pay yourself first.

What you do is you take your income and you set aside savings first and everything else that's left will be divvied up among expenses and liabilities. This is absolutely the correct way to do things. It's rough at first, it takes some getting used to, but the more you do it, the better you get at it. And I definitely congratulate you for having developed the discipline and personal financial skill to be able to pull this off.

However, as awesome as this accomplishment may be, it isn't enough. Saving is crucial for effective personal financial management, but simply saving or putting money in the bank is a losing game. Why? The 800-pound gorilla called inflation.

The Very Real Threat of Inflation

Before we get an understanding of why inflation is so bad, it's a good idea to talk about where inflation comes from. Why is it that the price of goods and services tend to rise over time?

Let's put it this way, if you walked into a Taco Bell 12 years ago, I can guarantee you that the prices on the menu look way different than their current price list. This is guaranteed. Why? Food

prices, just like with everything else, tend to go up over time.

Sure, there are certain categorical exemptions, but for the most part, this is true. In fact, this applies to almost all product categories. Whether we're looking at clothing, computer items, stereo equipment, and so on and so forth, the prices of goods tend to go up over time.

However, thanks to the outsourcing of manufacturing to China, a lot of the inflationary pressure on consumer goods have dropped fairly recently. It's anybody's guess how long this will continue. We seem to have gotten quite a bit of a break, thanks to the miracles of modern globalized mass manufacturing, which enables Walmart to sell products cheaper and cheaper by the year. That is the exception that proves the rule.

For everything else, especially services, prices tend to go up over time. The reason for this is due to money supply. You have to understand that unlike the olden days, the value of money is no longer tied to a physical object.

For the longest time, the value of the US dollar, as well as other currencies, was tied to gold or, to a lesser degree, silver. There was some sort of physical frame of reference for the value of money. While governments did play fast and loose with how they arrived at the value of their money or how they fixed the value of their money, for the most part, they still had a frame of reference that is tied to a precious metal.

Since there is that link to real world industrial value as represented by that precious metal, governments can't go crazy with valuation. They can't just print out money with abandon and expect the market to take care of it. It doesn't work that way. They are forced to establish some sort of discipline because their money is at least superficially backed up by gold or some sort of precious metal.

Well, nowadays, money only has value because the issuing government behind that money says that it has value. In other words, the global economy works on a "trust me" basis. This is why when global financial traders lose confidence in a government, that government's currency crashes. Look at the case of Zimbabwe for the most recent case study of this effect.

When Zimbabwe, starting in the early 2000's, started nationalizing white- farmer owned farms, it collapsed the economy. At a certain point, the Zimbabwe government was printing out notes in trillion denominations and it still wasn't enough to buy you a dozen eggs or a loaf of bread. If this sounds familiar, it is because this happens in almost all decades to many different economies.

For example, in the 1920's, this happened in Germany. People would take a wheelbarrow, fill it up with paper cash to buy a loaf of bread. This is the real problem with money that has no confidence. And unfortunately, when governments constantly print out billions upon billions of paper notes every single year, this has the residual effect of depressing purchasing value.

This is the real reason for inflation. It's all about money supply, as well as relative confidence in the currency, and the economy behind that currency. As you can probably already tell, there is a very real threat of inflation because it's always going up.

You have to find a way to protect the value of your money. Otherwise, regardless of how much cash you have saved up today, it's not going to buy much in the future because prices have shot through the roof.

Investing Grows Your Money

Investing grows the value of the money that you've saved up in the bank. That is the long and short of investing. The reason you're investing is because you want to end up with more than what you started. You also want to end up with more than what the bank will pay you in the form of interest.

You have to understand that keeping your money in the bank to collect interest is a losing game. Why? Not only is the interest pitifully low and always below the rate of inflation, you also get taxed on the appreciation of your money. In other words, you lose twice. That's why it's really important to make sure that you only put money in the bank as a temporary strategy while you're figuring where to ultimately invest your money.

Focus on investing your money instead of keeping it in cash form. Keeping your money in cash partially is always a good idea because you don't know what the future will bring. However, it is also always a bad idea to keep all your money in the form of cash because of inflation.

Investing enables you to grow your money. That is

the core of investing. With that said, there are different ways to grow your money.

Asset Classes

Asset classes are a fancy economic term for the different kinds of ways you can grow your money. You buy assets that differ from each other and these assets, categorically speaking, have different rates of appreciation. In other words, they grow your money at different rates.

It's important to note that when people talk about "investing," they almost always talk about stocks and bonds. But these two types of assets, as big and popular as they may be, are just two of many. You can try real estate, you can try passive income businesses, you can try active businesses, you can try precious metals. There are many different ways you can grow money, and this book will step you through some of the more common investment asset classes you can get into.

Anybody who is looking to transition from being a saver to an investor must first cut their teeth on the importance of compound growth. Compound growth works when you keep putting in money in your investments and they keep growing over time.

In other words, instead of just investing once in the past and forgetting about it, you continue to invest in consistent and constant increments so that your base of assets keeps growing and growing. Your older base appreciates to a certain degree, but this is followed up by a lesser appreciation for your more current investments.

If you were to add all of those investments up, they add to a lot more money than if you decided to invest a big amount last week. Why? Since your money has been sitting in the stock market or in the real estate market for a long enough period of time, it has appreciated considerably.

So, if you were to constantly put money in investments, the value of your money increases tremendously because you're making new investments, while older investments increase in value. In other words, you're simply building on the value base that you have built up from before.

This is why compounding is such a powerful force in personal finance. In fact, one of its biggest fans is Albert Einstein. With his massive intellect, he clearly saw the power of compounding.

The great thing about compounding is that it may start small, but as long as you're constantly adding to your investment, it continues to increase, especially if you do this over a fairly long period of time.

Different Ways of Measuring Investment Returns

Without boring you or scaring you with technical terms, I need to discuss with you the concept of "returns." When you first start investing, you probably are thinking that you just want to get more money than you put in. This is pretty basic.

If you are thinking along these lines, you are definitely on the right path. You know you are doing something wrong when you put in money in an investment and out comes less money than you put in. Most people can tell whether they're losing money or they're gaining money.

Now that you are clear that you want to gain money, the next step is to learn how to measure those gains the right way. Keep in mind that when you receive more money than you put in, this is called a return. This is a good thing. But this, of course, is not enough.

You have to be clear as to how to compare or judge the return that you get from one type of investment compared to another type of investment or another investment opportunity. This is where concepts like alpha and beta come in. While I'm not going to obsess too much about these specific benchmarks, it's important to note what they represent.

An alpha return metric is usually used in the stock market. The alpha measures the return on investment that you get for a particular stock compared to the index. Meaning, if you were to average out, with some adjustments, all the leading stocks of a certain collection of industries, you would get an average performance for the market as a whole. Your investment's alpha measurement clearly tells you whether the returns that you're getting from a particular stock is above average, average or below average.

While you may not be interested in investing in stocks, you should still think along the same lines. For example, if you are thinking of investing in precious metals or real estate, look at the return of investment that you're getting from those asset classes and compare them to the average within those asset classes.

For example, if you are investing in real estate and you've got into an REIT, look at the return of investment that you got from that particular investment compared to REITs, generally speaking, or better yet, the return on investment on the specific real estate market your REIT is invested in. This should give you a clearer picture of whether you are getting a good return or a mediocre one.

Keep in mind that just because you're getting more money than you put in, this is not enough. You have to compare it to something else.

Similarly, the beta metric measures how volatile your particular investment is compared to the market your investment is part of. For example, if you bought a stock, you notice the ups and downs of that stock over a certain period of time. Now compare how much it swings to the rest of the market. This is a good measurement not of return, but of risk. In other words, how likely is it for your investment to go from nasty to really heady upswings and nasty down swings.

This is a very important detail to keep in mind because not everybody can handle the stress of up and down-market movements equally. Some people are risk averse. They don't like risks. They're not big on surprises. Other people understand that the greater the risks, the greater the rewards. So, they're more tolerant of up and down swings.

Still, regardless of what asset class you're thinking of investing in, pay attention to beta or measurements of volatility because this can also guide you in buying certain investments within the same asset class that you feel are less volatile than others.

These two metrics work hand in hand. Alpha and beta must always be in your mind, not necessarily in technical terms, but instead, focus more on the ideas that they represent. Again, the return must be in the context of how the rest of the market in that asset class performs. Risk profile or volatility must also be measured by the general risk profile of the other assets in that asset class.

If you're trying to grow your money, you have actually many methods at your disposal. There are many ways to grow your money and end up with more cash than when you started. Investments are just one of them. You can loan out your money, you can put your money in savings accounts or similar instruments like certificate of deposits and treasury notes.

The Difference Between Investments and Loans

When you loan out your money, the person or company that takes out the loan (the borrower) is under legal obligation to not only give you your money back, but also provide a return for the money you loaned that person. This is called "interest." The amount you let that person borrow
is called the "principal."
Your profit in this scenario is, at least in terms of the law, is guaranteed. This person has no choice but to pay it back, unless the person goes bankrupt or there is some other legal reason that would justify that person not paying you back. Still, in terms of getting your money back, loans, at least on a superficial level, guarantee a return. The person has no choice but to pay you back.
Ideally, the best kind of loans involves the government. Basically, you issue a loan to a borrower, but the government steps in and guarantees that if the borrower cannot pay for whatever reason, the government will pay for the loan. This was

the idea behind the Fannie Mae housing loan program by the United States government.

Other governments have similar programs. The idea is for the government to enable people with low income to be able to afford homes. The ultimate guarantor of those loans is the federal government.

It's very easy to see why this is such a great deal for private lenders such as yourself. If there is a government program guaranteeing the loan, you don't have to worry whether the person who took out the loan can pay because the government will step in. Since the government has unlimited taxing power, unlike private institutions, you can rest assured that your money will return to you, plus interest.

An investment, on the other hand, doesn't have such guarantees. Whether a borrower is backed up by a third party or not, that person is legally obligated to pay you the principal, plus interest. When you invest that money, however, there is no guarantee that that money will come back. You just take a leap of faith that the investment will turn out well and you will not only get your money back, and a nice return.

Whether you're investing in stocks or mutual funds or real estate and other types of investments, there's always a possibility that you would lose your money. Even if you were to invest in a bond fund, for example, - a mutual fund that specializes in investing in bonds - you can still lose your shirt.

While bonds are technically loans, keep in mind that when you buy a bond from a corporation, that corporation can suffer hard times and be forced to declare bankruptcy. This does happen, and guess what happens to the holders of that company's bonds? While under the law, they get first priority to divide whatever assets are left by the company during bankruptcy, usually, the company has racked up so much debt and obligations that bond holders get only cents on the dollar.

Ultimately, the fact that you invested in bonds, in and of itself, does not give the same guarantees as if you had simply loaned your money to a borrower.

Investment Vs. Savings

When you save money at a bank or you take out a certificate of deposit or invest your money in a term deposit, the bank will guarantee you a published interest rate. This means that you get your money back plus an extra amount called the interest. Sounds good so far, right?

Well, the problem with savings interest-bearing accounts and certificates of deposits, as well as time deposits, is that the interest rate being offered is almost always lower than the rate of inflation. As mentioned earlier, inflation is constantly eating up the value of your money.

If you invest in an interest-bearing account, you are usually losing your fight against inflation. To add insult to injury, the government taxes whatever interest income you make off your money. Talk about rubbing it in.

Investments, on the other hand, are so varied and there are so many different options is terms of returns that you can take a calculated risk as to what kind of return you want. For example, historically, stocks have yielded an annual percentage appreciation of over 10%. Good luck finding that kind of return with a savings account or a term deposit account.

While there are very risky banks that would pay out higher interest rates, they only do so because there is a risk that they might go under. That's why they are highly motivated in getting people to deposit their money for long stretches of time. That's why they offer a higher than average interest rates.

The problem is that they also have a higher than average risk of possibly going belly up or otherwise experiencing a crunch that would prevent them from paying out interests. The great advantage of investments is that you tend to get higher returns compared to low risk savings programs.

Investments Vs. Government Instruments

The best investment if you are really scared of risk is, of course, the government. The US government and other governments around the world routinely issue bonds. These are basically IOU notes. They promise, that whoever bears those bonds, a certain return for whatever money they invest.

The great thing about government-backed securities is that the government is not going to go bankrupt any time soon. It can choose to raise taxes, it can choose to collect money in a wide number of ways, so funding, unlike that of a private company, is not an issue.

Now with that said, the drawback to government-backed loans is the possibility of default. While the government may default on their loans, they would still honor them, but the value of the loans would go down.

This is very rare and it usually happens to less stable economies, but it's still a possibility. Maybe the world experiences such a crippling financial crash that the US government is forced to disregard its loans or devalue its loans. It's a very remote possibility, but it can still happen.

On the whole, however, government-backed securities offer much more security to people who are terrified of risk. The downside is that there's so many people buying up government-backed securities that their interest rates or yields are fairly low.

There's really no incentive for the government to pay really high interest rates if it doesn't have to. This is especially true of debt instruments from the Bank of Japan. Japan is one of the most stable economies in the world and a lot of global investors buy up Japanese debt as a safe investment. When there's a tremendous amount of demand, the yields go down. Still, if you're looking for security and assurance that your money will come back, government-backed securities is definitely a good option.

Compare this with investments. When you invest, whether in stocks, bonds or private businesses, you have a chance of getting a much higher return. You may have invested an x amount of money and what will come back is that amount of money plus a nice return. Depending on what you invest in, the return might beat inflation, as well as the interest rate paid out by government debt. The downside to investing, of course, is that you can lose your investment. There is no guarantee that you will get your money back.

Chapter 7:

PRINCIPLES OF SUCCESS

Achievement is definitely the primary inspiration behind every attempt. The thrill that being successful creates is indescribable. In case you sample it the moment, it will not leave you, it can hold on for you, making demands for yet another rational ramification. Although the drive may be blamed as a little bit crazy, we have to get it. When you do not, who'll
get it done for you?
We have numerous teachings which tell how you can be a success. But how a lot of you became prosperous after looking at those? This is a good evaluation. I do not want to do some injustice to you as a reader. I purposely need to disclose the detailed
hypocrisy behind to help make the audience think.
This is the largest fault we come across in the current day. We are not approaching the question immediately. Someone wish to find out you in Bill Gates. Many others, wish to explain to you

the theorems of Alfred Einstein. Nonetheless, a great deal would like to help you move for any quantum jump.

But there is unanimity in all people. They altogether place the tongues in one mouth and show you to change the attitude which will point you to success.

Might I use the flexibility here to ask you one question - If I place you on Bill Gates' coat, are you going to be Bill Gates? To my little knowledge, the majority of the answers will likely be negative. As we genetically hate to be cloned.

I believe an evaluation of the term attitude is extremely pertinent here. It is convenient to say "change the attitude". But would you know the attitude is the one and the only thing making the person a private identity?

The method of the thinking, the manner in which you already know the planet, the strategy you feel this point is correct which thing is wrong, which merely causes you to completely different from others. If I take these from you, then your individual ceases to exist. This is the easy principle of nature. Must we stick to the principle of nature, or perhaps can I try and place you on another's trousers?

Go forward another step! You find the term feature. It can tell you a little lot. If you try to present a definition for the attitude, you notice it is strongly associated with the attributes.

Imagine what you are at this specific point of time? It is the sum total of the feelings, the pictures and the images you acquired on the good fabric of the brain after the birth, based on which you guide the actions.

This is the attribute, quite simply, the guiding scale for the attitude. What about a single facial morning a little body show you to change the attitude and you get the climb to Mount Everest. This not merely blocks you from good results, but additionally provide you with lifelong distress. We need to take every precaution to stay away from this tough situation.

Here's one way to help you move with all the attitudes. And that is the right way to see things. Nature isn't a small entity. An entity by virtue cannot add a limitation. It is hugely unlimited. It is perfectly made to provide you a room for success without tearing your attributes and attitudes apart which are the supreme markers for the personality.

Mimicking as art is good to look at. Though it is extremely bad to adapt it to the workplace and truthfully I will be the last individual to recommend such a thing.

I should direct you to success not by mimicking anyone, but by providing an obvious mention that you are not inferior to anyone. I do not trust or even believe that being successful is monopolized by an individual which it needs to go and then a negligent minority. It must be made available to others.

Because of this, we need just one thing. The determination.

This is the sole element that is needed in the journey to success. Determine today whether you would like to be successful or not. If perhaps the answer is "yes", then do not waste enough time to change the attitude sort of teachings. The following thing is perceiving it as easy as they can. Given that all it is an understanding of how to proceed.

It is amusing to determine how Einstein tackled a scenario which he finds extremely irrelevant to him. He has taken it with a humorous answer when asked the number of feet is located in a mile. The answer was, "I do not understand. Precisely why can I fill the brain of mine with facts?
I think it is in 2 minutes in every regular reference book." Einstein taught us a really great lesson that it is essential to work with the mind to consider instead of throwing needless numbers and facts the same as we place things in a factory.
The human mind isn't a warehouse to put numbers and facts to memorize later. It is received a far more easy and subtle feature of creativity that is the baseline for each success in this particular world. So now we have to ignite this particular faculty of imagination with the simpler understanding that I mention below:
Five steps to ignite the success one. Never undervalue your ability: Search always what is the specific thing in you that friends like.

1. Never overestimate others:

Think a new item you like the majority of. Don't actually compare the IQ with others

1. Develop a winning feeling:

Place yourself in good, creative work. Never bother about the damage. Say "I Am winning."

1. Search usually different and much better ways to do things:

Remember, the ability to think is better compared to the ability to memorize things.

1. Build actual, beneficial relationships:

A profitable man generally creates a lot of effective persons behind him. Success means a lot to people who believe and followed you. This puts the success a lasting nature, instead of a one-time element.

Last although not the least, we all have in one of the ways or even another worked out hard in achieving goals which we believed would provide us a lot and success of monetary and interpersonal clout.

However, in most cases, the strategy adopted point them to disengagement and so they include unrealized objectives & targets.

This particular approach that I describe here's a basic test, knowing the unbiased need of any common male, and it will make him not just to touch several sparks but additionally the fire of accomplishment itself.

Are you born successful people or can you become one? To be successful, is it essential to have a high social position or a substantial financial availability? Or maybe it's just a matter of luck? The notion of success is certainly very subjective, but to tackle this topic in a precise and scientific way, let's take as a reference the hierarchical scale of Maslow's famous pyramid of needs. The American psychologist Abraham Maslow, between 1943 and 1954 developed the concept of "hierarchy of needs or needs" which he represented on a pyramidal scale divided into five levels containing different needs: from the most elementary, necessary for the survival of the individual (such as for example food), to the more complex ones of a social nature.

The latter are the ones that refer to the most shared concept of "success", intended precisely as a social, work, etc. affirmation.

Volcanic motivation gurus and superstar trainers seem to hold the secrets that allow anyone to achieve desired success. But what are the methods to be successful in life that are scientifically verified?

Now let's see 7 ingredients that scientific studies have shown to be fundamental to achieving greater success in life.

1. *Increase Self-Confidence By Acting, Even By Clashing With Failure*

Katty Kay and Claire Shipman, authors of The Confidence Code, conducted a study on this topic, highlighting in addition to the existence of a wide trust gap between the sexes, that success is just as dependent on trust as it is on skills.

What was their conclusion? Low confidence translates into inertia.

"Taking action strengthens confidence in one's ability to succeed, so confidence grows through hard work, through success, and even through failure."

2.Improve your Social Skills

According to research conducted by economist Catherine Weinberger, of the University of California, the most successful entrepreneurs excel in both cognitive and social skills, although this has not always been true.

Every 10 years, the U.S. government examines a representative sample of high school students and tests them.

Then the individuals of this sample are followed for about 10 years to know the position reached in the world of work by the age of thirty.

Using these data, Weinberger cross-referenced a sample of adolescents from 1972 with that from 1992, concluding that:

"Smarter and more socially able people earn more in their jobs today than workers with similar skills in 1980".

3. Practice Delaying Rewards

In the famous marshmallow experiment conducted in 1972, a marshmallow was placed in front of a child, with the promise of a second marshmallow if he refrained from eating that greedy and fluffy morsel during the absence of the control researcher, which would last 15 minutes.

Follow-up studies over the next 40 years found that children who were able to resist the temptation to eat marshmallows had grown into people with better social skills, who scored higher on school tests and which there was a lower incidence of abuse of harmful substances. They had become people who had been able to achieve greater success, in short.

Furthermore, the former children who were able to resist marshmallows were on average in better physical shape when they grew up and much more resistant to stress than those who had succumbed to temptation as a child.

But how is it possible to improve our ability to delay things like eating "junk food" that we enjoy when we have no healthier alternatives available, or to keep running on the treadmill when we would rather just quit?

James Clear suggests starting small, choosing one thing at a time to gradually improve each day, and making a commitment not to avoid all those tasks that take no less than five minutes to complete, such as washing the dishes after a meal or eating. a fruit on a lunch break if we pursue the goal of eating healthy.

Committing to doing something every day also works.

The best in every field - athletes, musicians, CEOs, artists - are all more consistent than their peers. They keep their perseverance intact to carry on their routine, day after day, while all the others remain bogged down by the little big urgencies of daily life and the eternal conflict between procrastination and motivation.

4. Demonstrate Passion and Perseverance for Long-Term Goals

Psychologist Angela Duckworth has spent years studying children and adults, and has discovered the one trait that most significantly predicts success: it is grit.

"Having grit means taking on your future, day after day, not just for a week, not just for a month, but for many years, working really hard to make that future a reality. Grit is living life as if it were a marathon, not a speed race ".

5. Make yours be an open mind

According to research conducted by Stanford psychologist Carol Dweck, how people perceive their personality affects their ability to be happy and successful.

People with a "closed mind" believe that qualities such as character, intelligence and creativity are immutable, and the ability to avoid failure is a way of demonstrating one's ability and intelligence.

People with an "open mind", on the other hand, see failure as a way to grow and are therefore more likely to face challenges, persevere after failures, learn from criticism, and reach higher levels of achievement.

This does not mean that open-minded people believe that anyone can do and be anything, that anyone with the right motivation or education can become Einstein or Beethoven.

Rather, they believe that intelligence can be developed and that the true potential of a person is unknown and perhaps unknowable, so that it is impossible to predict what can be achieved by an individual through years of passion, effort, and continuous training.

6. Cultivate Personal Relationships

After following the lives of 268 Harvard University male students for decades, belonging to the classes from 1938 to 1940, psychiatrist George Vaillant's study has come to a scientific conclusion that you probably already know: love is the key to happiness. and therefore of personal success.

Vaillant found that even if a man achieves job success, earns a lot of money and is in good health, if his life is devoid of romantic relationships, he will never be happy and truly fulfilled

The psychiatrist's study has shown how happiness depends on two things: love and finding a way to face life that does not reject love far away.

7. Reassess Your Conception of Authenticity

Authenticity is a highly sought after component of personal leadership, and the prevailing idea is to consider the best leaders as those who are true to themselves and who make decisions based on their values.

Yet, in a Harvard Business Review article titled "The Authenticity Paradox" Professor Herminia Ibarra discusses an interesting research on the subject and tells the story of a newly promoted general manager who admitted to subordinates that she felt fearful of the responsibilities of her new role. , asking them to help her succeed.

Ibarra tells us that his sincerity failed dramatically. The new CEO lost credibility with the people who needed an authoritarian and resolute leader who could lead and inspire them.

So know that simulating the qualities of successful leaders does not make you a fake, it simply means that you are a "work in progress"

Chapter 8:

HOW TO FIND YOUR PASSION

Many of us live under the suggestion that passion can just be spontaneous and either you have it or you do not. Either you like the job or you don't. Possibly you like the spouse or you don't.

Possibly you like reading books or you do not. Possibly you like working out or you don't. Looking at all this, you might claim that passion could neither be forced nor produced.

However, this is simply not accurate. You can have a passion for a horde of things but really focusing on it and thinking about attaining several particular objectives you are enthusiastic about differs. You can create a passion for something provided you have patience and an open mind.

You can convert any typical act into an activity. Working reading, studying, could all be transformed directly into a passion. What is crucial is that a person needs to have the ability to locate the passion in life and you have to channel this passion into the proper things to ensure you can appreciate your life much better.

In case you are disappointed within your existing position, realize

that you can learn methods of leading a fulfilling life. To accomplish that, it is quite crucial that we fill life with clarity.

As it has been pointed out in earlier chapters, you can construct a fulfilling life by simply understanding and then capitalizing against your values, passions, and talents. Take the time period to comprehend yourself entirely - the greater energy you have, the more you can do to create passion in life.

Passion creates energy within you and good energy enables you to confront the toughest of the challenges. Creating a life that you are aiming for takes energy. The passions will give you the power and the motivation to carry out the work you have to accomplish heading in the path you most want.

We are enthusiastic about things which we care most deeply about. In case you are having difficulty waking up in the early morning and going to work, it is because you lack passion in the work.

In case you are powerless to sit down and share a meal with a partner, it is because you lack passion in the relationship. If you sit prior to the Tv all evening and don't care what fitness is similar to, it is also because you are not enthusiastic about health.

Use all the resources and tools we have discussed in this book to find out the passion and turn up the motivational levels. When you know and comprehend how you can bring about the passion of items that you need to and do care about then, you'll start enjoying life a lot.

You will be ready to prioritize much better around your passions and create a life that you simply enjoy. You will have a life which not merely works great for you but additionally looks great from the exterior.

When you have achieved the goals and realized the passions, what happens next? Effectively, sit down and chalk away another set of goals that you are enthusiastic about. And next, we need to get cracking!

There is a natural progression of achievement and success. It will take time, practice and effort to reach dreams and goals. When you get going, the activities get easier, which enables you to get more accomplished. You end up feeling good surges of energy and the confidence builds up. The energy and confidence fuel passion.

Do what is ideal for you making yourself happy and satisfied. Find passionate, kindred spirits. Together, you'll be exhilarated and energized by the fantastic fun and support you give one another. You will have an internal drive which will get you set up e morning, prepared to adopt e adventure with trust and contagious enthusiasm.

Make use of the following ten questions. Mirror throughout your whole life or career all the times you felt happy and satisfied. What were you doing? Differentiate the responses in between the activities if you felt easy satisfaction and those when you experienced fully charged and energized.

What core values and needs did these tasks fulfill? This awareness is going to help you figure out what could bring you passion today. The lists will help you decide what you have to bring into life.

How would you recognize what you are interested in? Consider the answers to the top ten questions for finding the passion. Continue Reading.

What do you want to do?

It does not matter who you are currently, just how much money you are making, what you have achieved in daily life, or just how great you believe you are. Until you have found the true goal of life, you are living a

lifestyle of mediocrity and haven't reached the potential. So why do a lot of people choose to sleep?

Because they are continuously tired or do not have anything else to do. How frequently will you come home exhausted, every one of the energy sucked from you and simply toss yourself before TV?

Many people seek out some people spark in life from entertainments, parties, friends. How frequently will you feel exhausted at the office when actually half of the day isn't over yet? You are tired, unmotivated.

And suddenly you got a phone call from a friend who proposes to do something cool in the evening. What goes on? You end up talking enthusiastically on the telephone, wave the hands, laugh - the tiredness appears to be swept away. Why the unexpected rise in energy? That is the power to do

things you love and are interested in.

In case you are not living the passion, you have a serious energy leak. Your productivity is down, you are depressed, stressed, and moody.

When you are doing something that is fun about which you are passionate, you feel a great deal of power. If you are not having fun, you are not performing the proper thing! This is wasting your energy and life. When the work is the passion, you won't ever work an additional day - it turns into an enjoyable exercise, an adventure.

We invest the majority of our waking life at the office. A lot of them at home, among our friends and family. What this means is the job is an important component of life. It has significance and its effect reach far beyond the income figure.

That can be happier, fitter and more effective in all facets of life, you have got to find everything you love and devote your life to it.

There is nothing much worse than spending the most effective years of everything stuck in a task that you do not love, understanding deep inside you that there is anything much better waiting available for you. Living favors people who show courage and do something to move their dreams forward.

So how can you begin?

Initially, you have got to discover what you are interested in. Write down the way you wish to feel. Begin with common intention. You do not need to get into small details, at least not at the beginning of the journey.

Visualize life when you are living the passion. The vision may excite you sufficiently to make you do anything about it. You have to create a choice which comes from the gut. The head is going to give you a lot of explanations why it is not a great idea, the reason you may fail and what judgments you will receive.

Emotionally, you may feel vulnerable and scared. You have to admit those messages, but ensure yours will prevail. You may not realize each step; you may not know if you are doing the proper thing or how you are likely to get there.

At this stage, after all the reflection, this is the stage that separates people who live the dreams of people who feel trapped. It is not knowledge, or insight or wisdom – It is the action. Take the leap. It is going to feel like jumping blindfold off of a cliff, though you need to have confidence in yourself.

To take Baby Steps

You have identified the direction, so take small steps toward it. Think of that fantasy life, just how much you need it and just how much you should have it and utilize that energy to dedicate yourself to taking a stride each day.

It might be small:

Emailing somebody who is going to be handy, taking on everyday trip someplace, establishing a meeting with important individuals or even businesses. It does not need to be groundbreaking, just be sure to keep the promise to yourself to do something every single day.

After ten days of doing this, look again at what you have performed and note just how much better you are today than before you made the commitment. Make use of the power you think from the success to catapult you through another ten days.

Remain True to Yourself

Success suggests doing work you find satisfying, work which causes you to happy, and living based on the values. Run your own race. Do not care what others say about you.

What matters is exactly what you inform yourself. If living the passion suggests doing the best that may be viewed from the

LEADERSHIP

typical and not aimed with "what individuals are claimed to do", the best risk of life isn't taking one.

Doing everything you really love doing is a procedure of self-disco" I believe the length of time the task takes will depend a great deal on the desire to find the solution. And yes it may be awfully scary wanting our own answers to what'll help make us happy.

Far too frequently we seek the guidance and direction from many other individuals. This is usually a terrible idea when attempting to discover what you will love doing. As loving others all around might be they have your own motives, ideas, and desires about precisely how we must live lives.

And since they believe the sun rises in the east and sets in the west does not imply that you cannot take a look at it as the planet trying to follow the east and subsequently the sunshine just coming into view.

Want to explain to somebody else what you will really like to be doing from the perspective is frequently hard. Nobody else is going to have exactly the same perspective on daily life and the significance of what you are doing.

Of course, if those individuals, particularly your family, never had the chance, or were discouraged from pursuing whatever they like for "practical reasons" they don't have any knowledge or ability about precisely how to help you in doing everything you enjoy. They might give you a simple response or call you a dreamer, if so, dream on.

But the dreams I am writing about are the type that comes up from deep within you. They are not really a process of the thinking that is the product of living.

Ironically performing everything you enjoy is the process of living by way of thinking. The dreams you would like as a kid, the dreams you nonetheless consider as an adult, are excellent signs about what you will like to be performing.

Consider all those ideas, all those dreams. Get a paper or 2 and begin to write. Put all them down. Do not stop analyzing them or pre-judge them, simply write them down. This first action is not around trying to decide, and figure out, what could work and what will not.

The next step is all about prioritizing the list. This is about doing everything you love. This is not around financial priorities, it is about life priorities. Presuming you will earn far more money settling for' this' fantasy rather than' that' one, that actually turns your crank, is a huge error.

When you are likely to do that you might want to stay working exactly where and for that are. This list and the prioritizing is all about life, not the living. Doing everything you really love doing, not doing everything you believe you can make the most money at.

Prioritizing the list is not about what you will love to be doing now and first second and third etc. It really is about narrowing the list of dreams to that one that should enable you to get growing and going in with the individual you would like to be, the person you currently are,. How can you begin' doing everything you love'? I believe the best option is writing it down as an objective.

Look at it each day for no less than a week and consider it. Then take a seat and write out a precise program for creating that life. Little simple steps that anyone can do, even though you, regardless of the length of time it might take. But be confident, being honestly committed to doing everything you enjoy in daily life can get you there quicker than you can wish for.

What Inspires You To The Maximum?

Ever thought about what motivates you the most or at the least how you can recognize precisely what that is you will be inspired by? Inspiration may additionally be at the surface level; it simply comes and goes,

providing you with nothing significant.

Discovering and finding what really motivates you will help you do something positive, as an outcome, even in the face of actual difficulty. Procrastination, depression, hopelessness, and indifference are the merchandise when you have lost hope and are confronted with the question: how you can remain inspired.

Hence, "how to determine what motivates you or could motivate you in life" is occasionally the most crucial question that you can solve. Finding something really inspirational becomes an uphill job. If done, no one is luckier than you.

Should you shop around, you will realize you'll find, actually, no fast and hard rules. Individuals can feel moved by anything available. Among the acquaintances of mine gets enthused by everything about him!

Somebody said "from the littlest sweet-tasting wrapper blowing in the breeze on the biggest building ad twenty stories high. Originating from a flame at a grill on the swell of the Irish sea; I really feel inspired by something I do not have any idea at this particular time."

Inspiration might additionally come just out of a great piece of advice; you might discover it from a book you are reading. Odds are that someone is going to go for probably the most essential decision of life only by listening to a portion of news on tv. You might undergo a comprehensive modification by watching a movie.

There is basically no cap regarding just how the thoughts, your vision or dreams will take a somersault most of an unexpected. It is a fascinating phenomenon that while commitment or a comprehensive change in the feelings might be brought on by an individual knock in the home, an entire bomb blast can go unnoticed of by someone in additional time.

Talented inspirational speakers are one more powerful source for groundbreaking changes. Right now there are souls that get carried away by the sight of money, or simply the thought of generating money by doing what just flashed throughout the minds.

Additionally, there are people that go crazy at the media that many Hollywood celebrity is likely to be around, which means they will have an opportunity to shake hands with or even purchase an autograph from a famous figure. The idea of using talents to help others also is inspirational.

There is much out there nowadays. You may feel inspired by individuals who struggle by starvation from daily. Are not there excellent designers around who inspire us at an excellent deal?

Whenever we glance at the list of all these kinds of conditions, great preferred choice or most sought after ones folks love to go after, it reads as:

A great cause and a life changing story; dream and desire of becoming a celebrity figure; longing to have sexual relation with somebody who lures you the most; money; higher education, a weather that is pleasant, a little poem, sight of a smashing developing, finding yourself in the organization of nature... and the list passes and on. The fundamental question, however also stays there: how you can recognize what motivates you in life?

The question, actually, has something to do with the core nature, the real self. It is that part of the personality which might remain hidden because of reasons that are varied, like adverse circumstances or your lack of showing adequate courage towards doing something you believe you can.

But anytime somebody does something of the same characteristics, you feel energized. No one around can feel as much enthused by that occurring as you are doing. Got it?

This is where your real interest and talent lie. To identify your passion, you simply have to find out what people type or happenings are excessively close up to your heart and mind. Provide it with a shot. You will quickly have discovered what motivates you in life.

What Makes You Genuinely Happy?

Consider this particular question, and I am not saying you need to simply think of a summary of mundane things which make you feel attractive, cookies, like flowers, or Christmas.

I am additionally not talking about the values or the love for those close to the hearts. For me personally, the supreme delights in life would be the loving moments I show all the individuals that enrich the experiences of mine. What I mean here's -

What activities and experiences do you have on a frequent basis that bring you joy?

I am talking about the type of happiness which

glows out from you and it is driven by the consistent actions. What would you do that brings you real joy?

You understand we utilize a lot of our lives filling up the room with things which we do though we do not actually have purpose or intention behind a lot of them. We are swept up in everyday. Wake up. Have several coffees. Go to work. Come home. Watch T.V. Go to sleep. Do this.

Remember when we were children, however. We have to accomplish all these things which brought us true pleasure, and we got to do them all the time. Just like playing with robotic toys or digging in the sand and blowing up our G.I. Joes with firecrackers or even playing an instrument.

We spent a lot of time playing and imagining games. We envisioned the planet how we wanted it to be. Whenever we were kids, we had been learning about ourselves. We had been studying what made us joyful.

Someplace, somehow, several of us got lost on the way to seeking happiness.

I think, for a lot of us, we might have just forgotten

how you can be curious about lives. What I mean by this is how frequently do we take time to sit back and consider the stuff we do or even utilized to complete that bring us pleasure?

This one has to take a fast moment, but go on and pull out a pen and paper - Jot down a fast list of 5 to 10 things that really bring you joy. This may be something easy that you can do now.

You might love singing one of the favorite songs or practicing ballet. It might be something which would take a little more time to achieve, such as going to find an area to do a little horseback going or riding golfing for the first time in years.

It might be that business start-up which you planned to begin for a long time and simply do not did it. It might blow up your G.I. Joes in a sand heap with firecrackers. Do not think deeply about this - merely jot it down.

Get curious about yourself. When you would like to believe in the dumping of passionate joy, definitely challenge yourself.

in case you cannot think of anything, answer this question - what might provide you pleasure if you are trying it. What might just make you glow within, in case you do not believe that pleasure in life right now, which ecstatic power from whatever you can think of, jot down items which may allow you to believe that way.

Just agree to this - every week do these activities. Jot it down in the schedule book, put aside the time and get it done! To make this more amazing, you can agree to do something each day that brings you that sensation of happiness and joy. It truly depends on everything you feel confident with, but begin this week and just get it done.

Whenever we put aside the time period to cultivate happiness and joy in lives, we have a great deal more light to talk about with other people.

Consider only a small amount of time every day to give to yourself and the light will brighten up a lot of better so that you might be a beacon of others. Which means you might be ready to talk about more joy with everyone you encounter.

In our contemporary society, it is often somebody else's goals we are trying to achieve. Our managers, spouses, and parents media frequently let us know what is expected of us. And quite often we still love it since it will keep us from being forced to look at a scheme ourselves.

But this is dangerous because sooner or later we may go to a point exactly where we instantly begin questioning if there should not be far more to life - to a lot of us this occurs close to the age of forty or perhaps so where most of life appears currently properly settled and we feel to be on a particular track that we can't change or leave any longer. Usually, the absence of self-awareness keeps individuals from discovering what they really wish to do and the way they wish to live in the first place.

Certainly, we want a particular degree of fiscal stability to follow a "normal" life but imagine concerning it: In case you did one thing you are great at and enthusiastic about, would not it be probably for the money to go by pretty much immediately after time?

Alright, this may not be correct for all situations and all passions, but perhaps in case you simply began to apply a little more of your passions and strengths in the current work environment, it may by now result in a substantially greater level of satisfaction, feeling and success of being connected to the job.

Thus, why do you not begin today and discover what truly drives and motivates you? What is it that could allow you to happy in the end? Next, move on and create your own agenda and stick with it almost as you can until you find a better path.

Everybody wants to be pleased. Nevertheless, a lot of people do not take time in thinking about the actual meaning of happiness.

Additionally, they fail to know the actual ways regarding how to attain it.

Getting new things like cars, electronics and clothes can make you happy, though they won't last for an extended time period. Once the personal things got obsolete, you will crave for more products making you feel happy once again. Just how can you learn the true long-term happiness and fulfillment?

Recognizing the real happiness is rather easy. All you have to accomplish is examining yourself, know the passion, and follow the heart. The primary question is, what steps are you going to take knowing the real passion? To understand the passion, just do the following:

Create a list - The most effective way to recognize your own passion is via the listing. Jot down all the items you wish to do, either big or small. In the listing, you do not have to limit yourself. Put anything so long as it brings happiness to life.

Ask yourself - What exactly are your desires and goals? You have to learn what causes you to feel satisfied and happy. If you are planning to do the job, what'll it be? When you respond to these questions, you are certain to have an ambition which will help make you feel contented.

Mix the talents - If you like singing and playing musical instruments before the group, then you definitely have to accomplish amazing tricks to astonish the audience. When you fulfill these actions, then expect that you will be satisfied and happy.

Never ever stop trying - In case you cannot find the passion, never quit trying. While you keep on trying, you'll quickly discover that best passion and achieve success. Success does not come easy. That is exactly why you have to be persevering until you achieve the goals.

Analyze The Passion - After understanding the likes, ambition, and dislikes, you have to think and analyze. You have to look for ways regarding how to achieve happiness. Say for example, in case the passion is traveling around the planet, then you have to generate more money for the daily expenses.

At this stage, you have to think about the ideal job that suits the qualifications. Right after earning adequate money for traveling, you can enjoy life each day.

Finding passion is the key to complete fulfillment and happiness to life. There are many ways regarding how to recognize passion. Imagine, dream and believe. When you do, you can quickly weigh the various things that you would like to do, whether it is big or not.

Everybody is free to fantasy, adhere to the heart, and pursue their passions and goals to attain their desired happiness. Whatever it is, you have to attain it accurately. Actual happiness won't ever be accomplished if you hurt somebody while going in addition to the success.

Make the correct decision and begin doing what you would like to do. It is the passion which would bring you happiness and never anything else!

LEADERSHIP

Chapter 9:

HOW TO HANDLE MONEY

Many people think that earning money and making money are the same thing, but like with most opinions about money, this isn't the case. In this chapter, we are going to look at what it means to earn money and what it means to make money. We are also going to look at which of these categories most people fall under and why making money is better for you than earning money.

Earning Money

When you are earning money, you are trading your time and energy for money. In other words, you work for an hour, and you are paid for an hour. If you do not work for that hour, you aren't paid. It doesn't matter if you are paid hourly, on a salary or commission. You are being paid by someone else in exchange for your time and energy. This means that you are relying on some other entity for the money that is going to support you and your lifestyle. Another aspect to earning money is that when you work for an hour, you are only going to be paid for that hour once. This is important to remember as we look into what it means to make money.

Making Money

When you are making money, you use your time and energy once and get paid over and over again. Making money allows you to be independent and doesn't require you to depend on someone else for the rest of your life.

People who earn money are often the ones who are in debt and are living paycheck to paycheck. Those who are making money are wealthy and have much more financial freedom.

The idea of putting your time and energy into something once and being paid for it over and over again may seem as though it is too good to be true. Here are a few examples of ways people make money:

• Coming up with an invention that they are able to sell to a person or company and receive an ongoing royalty;

• Writing a play that is licensed to a production company to turn into a movie or TV show;

• Investing in real estate properties and renting them out for more than the mortgage cost and other expenses;

• Investing in a parking lot and renting out the same spaces every day;

• Investing in dividend-producing stocks or other interest-producing financial instruments that pay out regularly.

This should give you an idea of the limitless possibilities that are out there for ways to do something one and be paid over and over again for it. Some people refer to this as passive income instead of earned income, but anyone who has invested in an income producing asset knows it is rarely completely passive. There is usually consistent work that is going to be involved in ensuring the asset contains to produce a regular income.

Do You Need To Earn Money To Make Money?

Some people believe that it takes money in order to make money. While this is true, it doesn't always have to be your money that you use in order to make money. You could be able to start making money right away if you are able to borrow the money by having Some people believe that it takes money in order to make money. While this is true, it doesn't always have to be your money that you use in order to make money. You could be able to start making money right away if you are able to borrow the money by having someone invest in your idea, or through a loan. This is referred to as leverage.

Leverage is when you are able to utilize other people's time, energy, and money to make you money. This could mean that you take your idea for a play to a play wright who hasn't been successful financially yet, and partnering with that person to get the play written. It could also be working with an investor to financially back your real estate deals when they don't have the time to find them, and you don't have the money to back them.

The downfall to using leverage is that you aren't completely in control of the process. However, leverage is a great way to get your money making career started.

Sometimes it doesn't take much money to create an income producing asset. Occasionally things might just fall into place the way you need them to and allow you to begin making money.

Why Is The Difference Between Making And Earning Money Important?

Eventually, you are going to be making enough money that you are going to be able to support your chosen lifestyle. At this time, you could choose to stop earning money. In other words, you can stop working at your day job and rely only on your "passive" income to support yourself. Alternatively, you can continue earning money until you are able to support both your chosen lifestyle as well as contribute to charities or community projects.

Making A Budget, And Sticking To It

In theory, making a budget might seem incredibly simple. Or the idea of a budget might leave you confused and frustrated. In reality, creating a budget can be confusing and frustrating, but it can also be incredibly simple. In this chapter, we are going to outline the steps on how to create a budget as well as cover some tips to help you stick to your budget successfully.

What Is A Budget

Before we get into how you to make a budget and how to use it, we are first going to look at what a budget is.

A budget is a written document or electronic file that is going to help you to take control of your personal finances. A budget is an excellent tool to help you manage your money and achieve your financial goals. A budget is a good idea for you if:

- You find that money is always tight;
- You aren't sure where your money is going;
- You are having a hard time paying off your debt;
- You don't save regularly; and
- You want to find ways to make your money stretch further.

A budget is going to give you a clear view on how much money you are bringing in, how much you are spending and how much you are saving. Creating a budget can help your find ways to eliminate your debt, reduce your spending, and have more money for the things that are really important to you.

Before You Begin Making A Budget

Before you start creating your budget, it is important that you know what your goals are as well as where your money is currently going.

Think About Your Goals – Take some time to think about what the goal of your budget it. Decide if you are trying to pay off your debts, have more money available, save for something, build a nest egg, go back to school. Your goal is yours individually, but it is important to have a goal in mind before you begin to create your budget.

Keep Track Of Your Money – Most people know how much money they make. However, what most people don't know, is where their money goes. Before you start making a budget, start tracking where your money is going. For one or two months, keep track of everything you purchase, from groceries to coffee. Keep a copy of all of your bills that you pay, and write it all down in a notebook. Doing this is going to help you understand your spending habits and put you on the path to success with your budget.

Making Your Budget

When you are ready to create your budget, you are going to follow four steps.

a. *Calculate Expenses* – The first thing you are going to need to do is calculate what your expenses are. You can use your bank statements, as well as the tracking you have already done to ensure that you are getting a clear picture. Since some things only happen every few months, or even once a year, it is important to go back through your records and make sure that you are accounting for everything. When you come to an expense that doesn't occur every month, take the cost of that expense and divide it by twelve so you can see your average monthly expenses.

Keep in mind that it is imperative that you are thorough when you are adding up your expenses. A forgotten bill is going to throw off your budget when it crops up. A good rule of thumb is to add an addition ten to fifteen percent into your expenses over what you have calculated. This means that if you determined that you spend
$1,500 a month, add $150 to $225 to that number.

a.   *Determine Your Income* – Once you know what your expenses are, you are going to need to know what your actual income is. While you probably know what your salary is, you will get a more accurate picture by calculating any extra income as well. This can include cash gifts, alimony, child support, interest, and rental income.

b.   *Figure Out What's Left* – Once you know your income and your expenses, you are going to be able to know if you have money left over, or if you are overspending.

If you have money left over, congratulations. You can now earmark this money for savings or pay off debt. If you find that you are spending more than you are making, it is time to make some cuts so you can save money and not go further into debt. This is where tracking your spending will come in handy. If you find that you are spending two dollars a day on coffee, this works out to fourteen dollars a week and seven hundred and twenty-eight dollars a year. This is significant when you are looking at ways to cut your spending. If you aren't able to cut enough of your spending, you should consider ways that you can increase your income.

a.   *Be Realistic* – When you are making your budget, be realistic with your numbers. Don't say that you are going to spend half of what you are going to spend on something. Doing this is only going to cause frustration when you are trying to stick to your budget. Be honest with yourself about where your money is going and what expenses you can cut.

Sticking To Your Budget

Making your budget is easier than it is going to be to successfully stick to it. While it is okay to fall off your budget once in a while, you want to make sure that this is the exception and not the rule. Below we are going to look at some tips on how you can be more successful at sticking to your budget.

Don't Carry Your Credit Cards Around – Availability is your enemy. If you are carrying your credit cards around, you are more likely to make an impulse purchase. This includes deleting your credit card information from your favorite websites.

Use Cash Only – When you are using cash to make purchases, you are far more aware of what you are spending. If you stick to using cash for all of your purchases, you can see when your money is gone. When your money is gone, you are stuck until your next budget cycle. This is going to lead to you being conscious of your spending choices, as you aren't going to want to leave yourself with no money to buy food.

Schedule A Budget Evaluation – Make time to sit down and look at your budget every couple of months. Your life is always changing and over time you might find that there are aspects of your budget that just don't work. Maybe you are making more or less money, or maybe your family has grown. Either way, it is your budget, and it is important that is works for you. Just don't lose sight of what your long term goals are.

Keep Track Of Your Money – Keep track of where you are spending your money. If you are finding that you aren't able to buy a number of groceries that you were expecting to, look at where you spent your money and what you spend it on. Knowing exactly where your money is going will make it easier for you to correct your budget and make it work for you.

Your budget doesn't need to be incredibly challenging. With a little patience and consistency, you will soon be sticking to your budget, and even find that you are coming in under budget some months.

LEADERSHIP

Chapter 10:

HOW TO MAKE AN IMPACT

Deciding to leave a positive mark on the world is a noble goal.

One of the most effective ways to find happiness, satisfaction, a sense of purpose and belonging is to try to improve the lives of others. However, this milestone can overwhelm you: How can you, one person, change the lives of others for the better? Thinking about this question can make you feel insignificant and helpless, but in this article you will find concrete advice on how to start influencing others in a positive way.

Find happiness

To make others happy, you have to start with yourself. What puts you in a good mood? What gives you joy? Answer these questions to begin understanding how to spread happiness to others.

Make a list of times when you have felt happiest. To help you remember you can browse a photo album. Pay attention to the images in which you seem happier or more peaceful: what did you do? Who were you with?

Can you still find time for those activities? If not, try to prioritize things that really make you feel happy.

For example, even if you no longer have the time to go for hours running in nature every weekend like you used to, you may be able to jog to the local park once or twice a week. You will be surprised how quickly your good mood will return after taking up an activity you loved very much.

Get your life in order

It is difficult to help others effectively if your life is chaos. If you really want to make a positive impact on the world, you will get better results if you are not too distracted by your personal problems.

Would you like to help the unemployed find decent jobs with insured pay? If you can't keep a steady job first, you won't be able to offer much advice and you certainly won't be taken seriously.

However, you shouldn't abandon your goal because you haven't been able to keep a high-paying job for a long time yet. When you succeed, you will be in an excellent position to help others like you.

Once you overcome the obstacles in your path, you will be able to

really understand the situation other people are in and offer them valid and proven advice.

Try to improve your life, not make it perfect

Even if the first step to helping others is to help yourself, be careful not to put off starting your path too long. You will never get to be completely happy, content, with the perfect job, etc.

If you wait for the moment to be perfect (and for your life to be) before you start making your mark on the world, you will never begin.

You may not be in a position to be an employment consultant, but you could provide homeless people with clothes to hold a job interview.

Identify your skills and talents

If you are trying to understand how you can make a positive impact in the world, you should get to know yourself as well as possible. Otherwise you won't be able to answer the question "What do you do best?".

For example, are you a person who organizes everything down to the smallest detail? Do you have a natural talent for public speaking? Are you very good at reading and writing? Can you program? Are you a football star?

Keep an open mind when answering these questions and don't rule out anything that seems silly or frivolous.

For example, you may be very good at creating complicated designs with nail polish and consider it a useless hobby.

However, nursing and retirement homes often seek out volunteers willing to manicure residents.

Think about the way you work best

Just as you should know what your talent is, you should also consider what kind of environment you express yourself best in. Answer the following questions to understand where and how to help others:

Do you feel more comfortable outdoors? Do you avoid bad weather at all costs and therefore prefer an office job? Are you an introverted person and therefore prefer to work from home?

Be honest about what you really like

In addition to knowing what your talent is, you also need to evaluate whether you enjoy doing the activities you are good at. To be able to help others consistently, you need to avoid boredom and exhaustion. To protect yourself from these problems, dedicate yourself to something you enjoy and excel at.

For example, you might be a great writer and use this ability to help others. However, if you hate writing, the chances of you keeping the commitment of teaching others to write are very low. Undoubtedly there are other things that you do well and that you like more.

Identify the causes that are important to you

Once your plan begins to take shape, you should think about what your passions are.

What causes are important to you? Are you a person who loves animals and would you rather interact with them than with people? Are you a staunch defender of women's rights? Do you passionately support the need for school reform?

Try to identify the causes that warm your heart or make your blood boil. Either way, you will know that you have engaged in something that matters a lot to you.

Decide how much time to spend helping others

Consider all your current commitments (work, school, family, etc.), in order to identify the moments of free time that you can dedicate to volunteering or doing good deeds.

Don't make overly ambitious promises about the time you can spend volunteering or working for others.

For example, if you promise to partner with the local animal shelter for 15 hours a week, they will rely on you, but after a couple of weeks you may lose motivation. You need to give yourself some time to relax.

However, you should prioritize helping others and setting that commitment on your calendar, as well as taking it as seriously as you do your job.

Find ways to help right away

In the noble mission of making a positive impact on the world, it's easy to look so far ahead as to ignore the opportunities that present themselves at the moment. Think about how you can improve the lives of others today.

You may be very busy and think you don't have time for anything, but you can still help with small gestures.

For example, you can set your alarm clock a few minutes earlier than normal and remove the ice from your neighbor's car before you go to work.

If you go to school, you can organize a study group before an important class assignment, or share your notes with a classmate who has been missing for a week from the flu.

Think about the little things that can help

Make a commitment to do good deeds every day. The best way to do this is to seek opportunities to spread joy and help others. Eg:

Keep the door open for people, making sure you do it with a welcoming smile.

Let someone who appears to be in a hurry pass in front of you when you are in line at the supermarket checkout.

Buy a pack of diapers for the new parents who live in the house next to yours (even if you don't know them).

Take a few minutes to cut out coupons from newspapers so you can buy more food and give it to the poor.

Frankly ask the service staff (waiters, shop assistants, gas stations, etc.) how your day is going.

Even if they are small gestures, they can have a big impact on others.

Look to the future

He continues every day to find ways to change the lives of others for the better, however small they may be. However, don't forget long-term goals as well.

For example, do you want to one day become a philanthropist or work for a non-profit organization? Would you like to work for Doctors Without Borders? Do you want to make sure that all children have adequate (and not only) learning materials at school?

Depending on your long-term goals, you may need

to spend some of your time already today developing and honing your skills, as well as acquiring the required knowledge.

This can mean that you will need to enroll in a particular course of study, get a job as an intern, or even change careers.

As a result, you will have to spend less time volunteering in the present, but you will become a tool that can improve the world in the future.

Consider your luck

Think about what you value in life, then find ways to spread that positivity to others.

For example, do you have a career today that rewards you thanks to the excellent education you received as a child? If so, you can express your gratitude and help others by providing the young people with the books they need.

Alternatively, you could offer free tutoring services for a couple of hours a week to children in the poorest areas of the city.

The basic idea is to understand the luck or help you have received and find ways to pass it on to others.

Chapter 11:

HOW TO START A BUSINESS

Starting a business from scratch can be simple if you know how.

Not the usual foregone words, but real principles that have made the fortune of thousands of entrepreneurs around the world.

Ready? Let's go!

Creating a business: the example of an entrepreneur.

In 2007 a simple Italian teacher decides to turn his life upside down. In spite of many Americans, he chooses to improve his way of life and the health of his body. So he starts running, playing sports, meditating. Finally, he gives up all his bad habits.

To increase his motivation, Leo decides to start a blog. He calls it Zenhabits, and begins to write down his goals, his discoveries, his accomplished results.

It is a real success. In just one year, the blog becomes the most important personal growth blog in the world, with hundreds of thousands of subscribers. In 2011 Zenhabits belongs to the top 10 most read blogs on the entire planet with more than a million subscribers.

With the publication of his ebooks and paid courses he has become extremely wealthy, and has thus funded many of the non-profit health and sports associations.

It goes without saying that he is now a legend. Especially for those who have the desire to start a skills-based online business.

17 Tips

Look for opportunities. Open your eyes and work hard to understand what people's needs and possible solutions to their problems might be. How could you improve the lives of others? What product or service could you give life to to start your online business and create your business?

If you can't wait to start, it means you have something good on your hands. Whenever I get the best ideas, I get super excited. I talk to people about it. I think about it at night. I can't sit for long from excitement.

Start small. People try to create a business and launch it in the biggest way possible. This is extremely wrong. Start as small as you can, perhaps by letting your friends and family try your product or service. Then have a few other people test. Always remember that the best advertising is word of mouth and the satisfaction of your customers.

The worst thing you can do is not to start. There is no worse failure than not even trying. If there is one nice thing about the web, it is that many ideas are achievable without expenses or with modest amounts. Trying is important, you will always have a chance to try a new idea again in the future.

Create a blog. The best way to advertise your business is to disseminate information and content for free. Show your willingness to give valuable content, help people without asking for anything in return, they will return the favor.

Don't do SEO, Social Media Marketing or Viral Marketing. This kind of thing has no value to people.

Rather it generates value. Build something good, and word of mouth will do the marketing part you need. Create valuable articles and content, and your blog won't need SEO.

Start learning. I started my online business with no money thanks to free or inexpensive services. Only after I made some money did I have the money to pay for anything or hire someone. Start making money as soon as possible by selling an ebook, a service, a product that has real value. Creating a business must be educational for you too.

Advertising is a bad business model. When you make money through banner ads, what are you selling? The attention of your audience, nothing more, nothing less! This is a very bad thing, and the people who follow you won't appreciate it. Instead, do what you can to delight your audience and get them to buy your product.

Forget about the numbers. More specifically, simplify your business and forget about achieving certain goals or targets. One million page views, tens of thousands of subscribers, half a million in revenues. Rather worry about how much you are helping your customers. How much value are you bringing to it? How can you make them happier? Before starting a business you must be aware that everything revolves around people.

Happiness comes quickly. A lot of people kill themselves to achieve certain goals, or to make a big pitch. Joy does not come from overcoming a goal, but from what you are doing to reach it. Be happy right away even for small satisfactions. Make sure you do something you enjoy, happiness will come by itself.

Forget about perfection. Too many people waste a lot of time trying to make their product, blog, site, launch perfect. It will never be enough. The pursuit of perfection can limit your sales.

Rather worry about trying, getting feedback, improving, and finally repeating.

What Is Financial Management and Why Do You Need It?

Financial management is about money. It is about controlling, monitoring, planning, and directing the use of funds in an organization. Whatever has to do with finance, from the petty cash tin to a billion-dollar public offering of shares, is part of financial management's remit. Unless you plan to pay your staff nothing, charge nothing for your products and services, and have no assets, you will need finance somewhere in the organization. And you'll need to manage it. So really, there is no escape from financial management – if you ask "why do I need it?" you might as well ask "why do I need to breathe?" or "why do I need to eat?" You just do!

On the other hand, why do you need *good* financial management?

Because if you don't have good financial systems, you are not fully in control of your business. Imagine two beer festivals, both running for a week. One has a report of how much beer has sold within fifteen minutes of closing. The other doesn't record what has sold. Which one do you think has the more chance of running out of beer without having reordered? Which one has the higher chance that it will end up with a lot of wastage?

Many start-ups have a tough time when they want to raise funds for growth. They have been going for a couple of years, but venture capitalists or bankers want to see figures that break down their activities in greater detail – and they don't have them. Or the figures they do have are somewhat approximate. It makes life much, much easier if you have good financial management from the start.

Good financial systems let you make smart budgets. Instead of just trying to increase all sales or cut all costs, good systems will help you identify those areas where you can make the most impact.

Good financial systems let you see how you are doing. If margins take a dive, or if your sales in one area are running away, you can see straight away, and take corrective action, or divert more resources to support your success.

Good financial systems help 'police' your business. You will see how well each branch is doing, and you can see if something is going wrong, whether that's a simple mistake (one retailer caught a store where a member of staff had managed to print out all the $99 labels as

$9.99!) or theft or fraud.

Good financial management will help you make sure your business is well capitalized and has the right financial structure. For instance, if you deal with long contracts and project payments that can stretch several years into the future, you need to have a good equity base and long-term financing – or, perhaps, you could look into trade finance. Otherwise, you are going to find your finances stretched whenever you have outgoings, but none of

your projects are reaching milestones this month.

Good financial management makes sure your customers aren't taking advantage of you. Too many businesses have been forced into bankruptcy when a big customer goes bust and hasn't paid its bills. A well-thought-out credit control policy, together with good reporting systems, should flag up any issues before they become critical.

A great product or service is a wonderful thing. However, a great *business* has to add more to the mix. It has to add marketing, of course, so that customers get to know about the product and want to buy it. But it also has to add financial management, so that the business is supported by financial resources, and can put those resources to the best use.

You won't *start* a business by applying financial management. However, it is financial management that keeps it healthy and growing.

Buying or selling a business

SELLING

If you're selling a business, one of the things you need to think about is timing. Remember that there are stock market booms and stock market busts, and that valuations change because of the market's movements, but also because of changes in competitive conditions.

You may also have your own timing to think about; when to make the transition to the next generation of a family firm, when to retire. It's important not to miss the boat - if you wait five years to sell, but the industry is no longer looking as optimistic as it did at the start, you might actually get less for the business the longer you hold on.

Don't miss the boat. An expert witness on valuation remembers a divorce case that happened about the time of the tech market crash. The main asset in dispute, on which the witness had been asked to deliver a valuation, was a VPN company that the husband had set up and developed into a major provider. It started at a value of about $50m, but the wife kept challenging the husband's figures. By the time the couple got their divorce, the value of the business was down to just $2m.

Another cautionary tale also comes from the tech sector. Myspace sold out to News Corporation in 2005, when it was the biggest social networking site in the world. It was valued at

$580m. But by 2008, it had been overtaken by Facebook. In June 2011, News Corp sold it - for just $35m.

Coming right down to local level, even though valuations might not see the kind of dramatic swings that the tech sector has seen over the last two decades, you can't take a successful sale as a given - particularly if buyers depend on bank finance. A bookshop owner with a huge stock of second- hand books wanted to retire. Five years before, he'd had a good offer for the shop with all the stock and the living quarters above. He didn't take it. Now, he found no one was interested in the business. One or two people made enquiries, but couldn't raise enough finances to take the business over. The shop was worth more if he sold it for conversion to a house. He got his retirement fund, and in addition was able to warehouse the stock and trade on the internet. But he had always wanted to pass the shop on as a going concern, and was sad that he wasn't able to.

So if you're aiming to sell a business, start the process early. For instance, start getting your documentation in order. Tighten up the book-keeping and if you want to sell a part of the business, start producing separate financial accounts for it. Clean up any 'dirty laundry' - make write-offs on obsolete stock, for instance.

Deals take time. Even selling an apartment can take several months; businesses are more difficult to sell and can take over a year. Buyers will normally want to do their due diligence, or to send their accountant to do it; if you don't have the numbers they want, it could take extra time to produce the right information. You may have two or three potential buyers. Negotiating the price takes time.

Get started well before you need to sell. If you want to retire in five years' time, it's not too early to start thinking about what the business is worth, what could make it worth more, and what could help make a quick and orderly sale.

If you find a buyer, you need to do *your* due diligence by assessing their ability to pay. Are they spending cash, or depending on a bank loan? Have they started talking to their bank, or will you need to allow time for them to do so? How sure are they that they'll get their finance - do they have personal assets that they'll use as collateral? Buyers who bridle at this kind of questioning may just be prickly - but equally, they could have something to hide.

Make very, very sure that you do your due diligence if the buyer wants to issue promissory notes or give you shares at part of the deal. And if you get shares, beware of lock-in periods and other restrictions on sale.

BUYING

As a business buyer you'll need to do due diligence, or, in more vulgar parlance, 'kick the tyres'. Quite a lot of it is about checking that the numbers in the accounts are real - adding a quality assessment to the quantities shown. Here are just a few of the ways
you might do your due diligence.

Spot-checking customers. Talk to customers and ask them when they first bought from the company. If there don't seem to be any new customers in the last five years, beware! Equally, if the company's been going for ten years but none of the customers you speak to have dealt with it for more than six months, is there something going wrong that you should know about? Also ask customers what other suppliers they use, and try to get a feeling for how easily they could move their business if they wanted to.

Checking stocks. A physical inventory audit will turn up signs of obsolescence, or of slow moving, older stock. Are stationery cupboards full of old posters and unused marketing materials? Are
there heaps of cardboard boxes in the back of a loading bay? Keep
an eye open for any signs of theft or 'skimming'. See if you can work out what's being paid for stock and if it's normal for the industry - buying too dear and selling too cheap is a sure way to disaster, but more importantly, some hotel bar managers have been known to cut a deal with their suppliers. They pay 150% of the market price for all their spirits, and pocket half of that themselves while the supplier still gets an inflated price.

Checking the plant and equipment. Is it kept in good order? Has it been well maintained? Is it in use? If you see plant that's mothballed, or that's not working when you visit, find out why.

LEADERSHIP

I often get asked how you can judge the state of equipment if you're not an industry specialist. It's not that difficult, though. A meeting of bank staff a few years ago turned up some wonderful stories of 'the worst plant I ever visited'.

One junior banker was on a tour of a small specialised foundry. All the furnaces were lit, and the workers were clearly busy, from the amount of noise they were making. This guy needed to use the bathroom, and took a break from the tour. On his way back to rejoin the group, he noticed most of the furnaces were dying down, and the workers had all disappeared. There was, he told his boss, definitely something wrong with the accounts.

That's nothing, another investment officer said.

She'd visited a factory where the overhead conveyor kept dropping product on the floor because the grippers didn't operate properly. Fortunately, no one actually got hit by falling glass , but when she added up the accidents she'd seen, she reckoned that a quarter to a third of the product never reached the end of the production line. No wonder costs were the highest in the industry!

But a third guy had the best of all stories. He visited a business that was supposed to be making precision instrumentation. True, it did have a few micrometers and dial indicators on show, but it turned out it made most of its money making kids' toys,

Keep your eyes open and your wits about you, and above all, do the legwork

- and you'll be protecting yourself against business disasters like these.

Take a good look at the products and where they are in the product lifecycle: are they developing, or are they mature or declining? Will they need marketing investment to kick-start them? A good example here is the craft beer movement. Beers from the first wave of craft breweries became 'old news' as new styles like sours and 'juicy hazy IPAs' arrived, and some of those first wave breweries have now ceased trading.

If it's relevant, look at the research pipeline. What new products does the business have coming along? If there's nothing new on the horizon, in a tech or fashion dependent industry, that could be bad news.

Check if a business has had any insurance refused. That's a big red flag. Many retailers that have hit the skids were first refused trade credit insurance.

Check contracts with suppliers. Are supplies secure? How much can suppliers increase prices? Check rent agreements - can the rental be increased? How does it compare with other similar property?

Check service agreements with customers and most importantly, in any service business which has formal service agreements, check if there have been any breaches and how much that has cost. How large a penalty will the company pay if it can't keep on track of major projects?

Check the payroll. Does it all add up to the number in the accounts? Are employees getting paid market rates? Less, and you could have a problem recruiting - more, and someone's feather- bedding.

Check the sales turnover against real world common sense. You can even 'go undercover', or have someone do it for you. One junior equity analyst camped out for the day in a cafe opposite a factory gate to count trucks going in and coming out. His day netted him a fat bonus - he'd worked out there was no way the factory was making the numbers that the boss had said it would.

Check title (Does the business actually own its premises, or rent? Do the same with intellectual property.)

Check zoning / land use / planning permissions, and any environmental regulations that could increase business costs. Never trust a business owner to tell you all of this - he may not know! Many small production businesses get started as an artisan working in a garage - when the business grows, it stays in the garage, and hey, isn't that against the regulations? That might have worked okay for the original owner, but you should be very careful about investing money in this situation.

Check for any pending lawsuits. Litigation can destroy a business's value. (It could also mean you are better off simply buying the business assets, rather than buying the business.)

Take a look at similar businesses in the local area, if relevant - are there more starting up, or closing?

Sometimes the decision on whether to buy a business is a very personal one. A small tech company was for sale at what looked quite a bargain price, but two things niggled. One was that the chief technology officer somehow never seemed to be available for a meeting. The other was that the CEO really didn't seem switched on to technology; he needed to ask his secretary to print out his e-mails and couldn't use the remote control on a video.

But even so, the deal didn't actually die until the CEO, when asked about projections for the total share of his business, said "Guys, this will be bigger than the internet. We are actually going to replace the internet."

If the owner of a business looks like a fantasist, or seems to have missed a trick - like a fashion brand that has no social media policy - then you should be worried.

Chapter 12:

THE IMPORTANCE OF TRAVEL

Travel is knowledge

Knowledge of new cultures, customs and traditions, of places, people and lifestyles. Traveling means discovering the world and not limiting oneself to one's own reality, be it provincial or metropolitan, broadening the mental and physical horizons to forge our identity.

The importance of traveling lies in the path you undertake, the goal is not important but how it is reached.

Meetings, exchanges, experiences, paths and goals enrich our personality and allow us to consider the world from different perspectives. There is no worse limit than ignorance, understood as not knowing the other, the different. The world is an immense chamber of wonders!

Traveling opens the mind and soul, because traveling is living and a life without travel is like a flower without petals. Since the origins of the world, travel has represented the human being's insatiable curiosity for the unknown, a search for the other who is different from himself but also a search for oneself.

Only by traveling is it possible to be aware of the multiplicity of worlds, ethnic groups and cultures that characterize our planet, making it extraordinary. The importance of traveling also lies, and perhaps above all, in all those emotions and perceptions that a trip arouses.

When you travel, you discover sides of yourself that you never thought existed: you can feel fearful, courageous, curious, adventurous, instinctive, methodical, passionate, rational, insane or hungry

for new experiences.

When you travel you realize that you are an individual among billions of individuals and you understand that, most likely, your ideas are not as absolute as you have always believed. You learn to appreciate the little things, even those that you took for granted or didn't even deserve your interest.

When you travel, you value individual moments and are able to enjoy them, you understand that life goes beyond the daily routine and you feel wonderfully alive.

The importance of traveling is knowing, going beyond one's limits, searching for oneself, experiencing new emotions, meeting people, discovering new places and cultures, testing oneself, appreciating what one has, accepting diversity, opening one's mind, and who the more he has the more he puts.

Most people think that we are all capable of traveling.

Who is it who doesn't know how to take a plane and go to any place on the planet, stay for a while and come back?

In reality, traveling is an art and in order to distance yourself from the much simpler activity of going on vacation, you need some specific skills, good doses of awareness and a little experience in the field. You can understand the difference between simple movement in earthly space and travel when you need what you put into practice while you are away from home even when you return.

Creative activities are expressions of oneself, they emphasize the combination of various elements, the infinite possibilities. Traveling is one of these: the world offers its colors and you compose them in your own way, a real work of art in which you end up finding yourself. It can happen in a remote hotel room on the edge of the known world or on the busy streets of a large and famous metropolis. While on a rickety bus or on the slopes of Sinai. It doesn't really matter where. If you travel, it happens sooner or later. And it is in that precise moment that you understand the scope and importance of the journey.

Today, traveling is almost within everyone's reach

More and more people are traveling, according to statistics recorded by World Travel & Tourism for example, in 2014, China was the first country of outbound tourists (about 120,000,000).

LEADERSHIP

According to John Steinback, "people don't take trips, trips make people". They shape people, in fact, when the latter (people) return they are no longer the same, because they "grow" from a cultural, social and moral point of view. After all, if we think about it, life is nothing more than an infinite journey to discover what we do not know: places, traditions, foods, people, customs, customs, cultures, and, most importantly, "ourselves". When we travel we open up to the world, we broaden our horizons, we learn to distinguish what is right from what is wrong, to understand who we really are and who we want to be. Traveling allows us to change perspective, to look at the world with different eyes and to know how to appreciate our things more. It also "materially" unites the world, since it allows you to have relationships between various ethnic groups and to deal with them, which is very important in the workplace. As far as young people are concerned, traveling has a fundamental role, since "traveling is the best way to learn", so, dear parents, if you have the opportunity, do not be skeptical about sending your children abroad, because it is the best gift you can give to your children, not so much for the happiness of leaving and getting to know new places, but for the wealth of information they will acquire.

"Life is a journey, and those who travel live twice," says Omar Khayyam. You can also do it by reading a book - "traveling with your imagination" for example - but the difference is that in that way you have imagined everything, instead you have lived while traveling, you have touched the architecture of the various places and have certain memories. of your experience and what it has passed on to you.

There are several reasons that lead man to travel, it may be the need to escape from the usual routine, to relax, to "pamper"; or it is curiosity that pushes man to go to destinations that are perhaps little known, wild, to make new adventures and to enrich his knowledge. Whatever the motivation of the trip, it is an experience that, perhaps once in a lifetime, we should all have.

Why travel?

Have you already asked yourself this question? For me, traveling is something natural, important and also instinctive. Here are the benefits of a trip:

Learning languages

I will not dwell much on this aspect, you are certainly already aware of the importance of learning foreign languages (it's also good for your health!)

To learn a language, one of the best ways is to stay abroad in order to practice. Such an experience is an accelerator, it saves time in learning. Best of all, it's the funniest way to learn!

Before you leave, don't forget to learn or review the basics to get by on the journey. MosaLingua has created a series of apps that allow you to get away with it quickly when traveling abroad. I also recommend that you download our conversation manuals for free, available in English, Spanish, German, French, Portuguese, which contain the essentials you need to know before leaving.

In addition, learning a language is also learning a culture and another way of thinking. All this can be learned by living among people!

Broaden your vision of the world and life

Traveling has changed my way of seeing the world a lot. Nothing more normal, since the journey allows you to broaden your knowledge.

Traveling means seeing other cultures closely, realizing that, in life, we share the same fundamental values and the same goals. We are part of a whole, we are all connected. What's better for

learning tolerance?

When you return home, you will certainly be more tolerant of others, especially foreigners. We are often afraid of what we do not know. You will also face life's difficulties and small daily problems with greater detachment.

Greater self-confidence

It is even more true if you leave for the other part of the world. Clashing with other cultures and with different environments can only strengthen our self-confidence.

If you are shy, traveling can be of great help! Forget the € 100 an hour coaches who promise to help overcome shyness, they are certainly not worth a trip.

You will go more towards others. It will also become natural after a certain period. And who knows, maybe you will also become a great talker!

Live strong experiences

That's what travel offers. Provided, of course, to look for it. The choice is as big as the world.

Traveling independently means making often strong encounters. It also means discovering incredible sites, landscapes from another world, mythical places. Traveling is having the opportunity to do activities that otherwise we would never have had the opportunity to discover.

And the money to travel?

Many people think that travel is expensive and when you tell them about a long journey, they roll their eyes and say "Impossible for me, I would never have enough money".

Traveling is expensive, here is a true urban legend that lasts to die! This myth is, moreover, well kept alive by the tourism industry. Between us, it is in their interest: their purpose is to sell organized trips

at a weight of gold!

When I started traveling 15 years ago, I certainly didn't imagine all the possibilities there are for cheap travel.

Along the way, there are tons of tricks and techniques to cut costs. Not to mention all the aids and programs available! There is also the possibility of being paid to travel!

And then, you can even work on the go! There are tons of opportunities! Finally, there are also several alternative ways of traveling: volunteering, woof and the like, traveling on foot, by bicycle....

What you may be missing is information. If more people knew all the possibilities, they would undoubtedly travel more.

We conclude by quoting the beautiful words of Paulo Coelho: "The world is in the hands of those who have the courage to dream and run the risk of living their dreams".

Chapter 13:

HOW TO COMMUNICATE WELL

For some of us out there, speaking to someone in a casual atmosphere may be easy, while speaking to someone in a more forced social situation may make us more inclined to hide from the world than anything else. There are also instances where we fumble over our words, overact, fidget too much, say inappropriate things, or feel we need to fill the silence by saying something.

Or perhaps, it's as simple as being shy or having social anxieties. Learning the basics of communication is only part of your journey to improve your social skills. The other parts are for you to understand what your goals are and for you to actually put them into play.

There are three basic communication areas we'll be going over. These are non-verbal communication, basic social skills, and real-world application. Non-verbal communication normally deals with body language which accounts for 55% of effective communication, while the verbal aspect accounts for the other 45% by splitting them into separate categories: the tone of voice and words. Your tone of voice accounts for 38% of effective communication, while the words you and others say are the lowest at only 7%. Now, why do you think that is? Why do you think we pick up on someone's body language and the sound of their voice more than what they're actually saying?

It's because unspoken forms of communication are universal. They go back before we learned how to talk and when we knew what words were. These are the first things we come to understand at a very young age. When a baby laughs, it must mean it thinks something is funny. When a baby cries, we instinctively think something is wrong. When we speak lovingly to a baby, they begin to respond not only to the voice but to the action that follows. In short, you can say this has been programmed into us since a very young age. This is something we have taught ourselves to recognize comfort, safety, and nourishment. As this is the very first thing we learned, we unknowingly take it any indication of that safety and comfort from the people around us as we get older. We see gestures before we speak. We hear the tone before we listen to words. We understand the other person's message before we get involved with the conversation. Just by visually assessing and by understanding the tone, you get a notion of how this person may feel.

In addition to these non-verbal aspects, there is listening. Listening is actually a form of communication; however, we'll be focusing on Active Listening.

This art of communication requires the listener to be engaged in the conversation by having your ears open more so than trying to convey or fill in the silence with words. This actually is very important to those who are trying to connect. They want someone who is going to listen and understand their message. If you're the quiet type already, then you're already there; not because you're silent, but because you know how to listen and observe overall. Staying silent can tremendously work to your advantage at times when used properly.

In order to help you build a genuine rapport with others, active listening gives you the advantage of understanding your partner or group members more easily. This opens up opportunities to chime in with some nuggets of wisdom after they're done. This shows others that you're willing to listen to what they have to say, relate, and not judge but help if need be. For you, this builds trust between you and whomever you speak with. However, if you're the nervous type and still find yourself struggling with social situations like these, here's some advice about active listening.

Active Listening is where you listen for the sake of understanding, not for replying. Many people only stay silent in order to build a rebuttal, but if you're trying to get people to like who you are, it's best to understand what they're trying to say, instead of spending energy and nerves scrambling for something to say in exchange. You want the others to feel safe around you and open up possibilities to meet up in the future. To be a good listener, don't judge. Let people talk and engage with them in their moments.

As you're listening, take note of how they sound. Do they sound happy? If they do, then perhaps what they're saying is going to lead to something funny? Do they sound disappointed? If they do, then perhaps you should offer some feedback by relating to a similar situation you once experienced? Do they sound irritated? If they do, then perhaps lending some advice to help them see a silver lining will help? Regardless of what you are listening to, always save what you want to say for last. To make sure they're done speaking, just wait for them to fall silent. You can say things like "Well," or "You know what," after you've listened and understood what they were trying to say. As someone meeting others for the first time, don't feel as though you can't say what's on your mind, just remember there are appropriate and inappropriate things that will either have you liked by others or ignored.

Let's talk about Body Language again. As mentioned, body language accounts for 55% of effective communication. This is your first step in determining the direction of your conversation and even understanding if the other person is engaged or not. This should also be something you're mindful of when speaking to others too since you are also part of this conversation and trying to make an impression. A person's body language is based on their personality. For you, you want to use positive body language, not body language that tells others that you're not interested, scared, fidgety, or have an anxiety. The non-verbal movements and gestures convey messages of interest, enthusiasm, and positive reactions to what others are saying. If you want to make sure you aren't hurting your chances, try making a checklist of what to look out for.

Body Language

Eye contact - With your head up, try to keep eye contact. Remember, don't stare, but causally blink. Staring will give people the impression that you're creepy, someone to watch out for, and avoid.

The handshake - Make sure your hands are dry. Damp hands aren't good for a first impression. So, on that note, just remember to breathe and understand that they're probably just as nervous as you are. Calm down, take a deep breath, and shake with a firm, yet confident grip. Naturally, if you're around your friends, you have your own greeting. However, for first-time meetings like this, it's important to solidify respect and confidence first.

Your posture - Your posture says it all. If your shoulders are slumped forward, your eyes are focused on the ground or floor, and you speak in muttered-quiet tones, then you're not about to make a good impression. You just told the person you're in front of that you don't care and you feel forced just by being here. By doing so, you've cut this conversation very short. A person trying to speak with you will no longer do so and will make sure to not include you in future conversations. So, always make sure that your posture is relaxed in either sitting or standing position, your back is straight, yet not stiff, and either slightly inclined forward or completely facing the one speaking. This shows they have your full attention.

Your arms and hands - Where your arms and hands are is also a giveaway. Are they stiff at your sides? Are you playing with your hands due to nerves? Are they stuffed in your pockets? When engaging in a conversation with someone else, your arms and hands should be involved with the conversation.

The arms should not be stuck stiffly to the sides of your body but opened comfortably at the sides. Using hand gestures to illustrate your story is okay to do as it shows engagement. Even if you're already holding something, that's okay too. Try to maneuver what you're holding to one arm as you speak. This shows interest, a friendly demeanor, and a willingness to be in the company of the other person.

So how do you read the body language of another person? Well, here are some examples of what to look out for. As mentioned, body language is based on an individual's personality. So, the more you understand this person, the best you can interpret their body language. However, the list provided will be for the occasions where you're meeting someone for the first time. It can also be applied to those moments where you're on your way towards getting to know who they are.

Reading Body Language

Someone's good posture is a strong indicator of confidence, their power, and the level of their engagement. If the posture is slouched as discussed, this decreases their presence for engaging with you and reduces the space for you to speak to them. A person holding themselves like this could be seen as a weakness. The crossing of arms and legs could be a sign of resistance. What is being resisted isn't something that's very clear. Sometimes, the indication is the conversation. Perhaps you're making them feel uncomfortable. Or maybe they're not feeling well, they're fidgety, and trying to focus. It's not very clear unless you give them room to talk about where they want to be right now. Be careful though, since this stance is also a sign of defensiveness and maybe give you guarded answers. In addition to this, they can be emotionally shutting you out. If their hands are clenched, they could be irritated, angry, or nervous. So, if you encounter this kind of body language, tread carefully until you either understand the situation or decide it's best to depart.

When someone is smiling and laughing, it's clearly because they're having a good time, right? Just remember, sometimes this could also mean they're nervous and they're trying to deflect from it. Sure, laughing, and smiling is good, but only in context. If someone tells a joke and everyone laughs, then you know why. However, if their smile seems to be glued to their face and their laugh and body language do not match, then you know they're nervous. So, in this instance, say something you feel was goofy in your life that you don't mind sharing. This helps alleviate that person's tension and helps break down their "nervous" personality barrier in order to help them feel more comfortable. So, if you see someone with a clenched jaw, stiff neck, or a furrowed brow, this could mean they're too serious, under stress, and/or uncomfortable.

Knowing what a person's eye contact means is also important. The average time one should maintain eye contact without staring is around 7 to 10 seconds. If the conversation is really engaging, then the contact may be a bit longer. Just remember you're not staring at them, you're maintaining interest. Staring would make those around you feel uncomfortable, just like if one were to start darting their eyes from side to side, or look into an empty space. These are normal signs of discomfort, as well as signs that someone may be lying or just distracted. Heck, if they're always looking down and away, they could simply be shy. No matter what version of body language you run into, remember that you're there to socialize and feel comfortable doing so. If you're too busy trying to read into their gestures or moods, then you're also neglecting the time you could be using to be an active listener. Also, what do active listeners do?

They don't judge. They're engaged and they wait till the person is done to relate.

Let's talk about your tone of voice. Once again, tone accounts for 38% of effective communication. However, there are other aspects to one's tone to clue you in on how the conversation will feel and likely the temperament of the person you're speaking to. These four aspects of communication style are Passive, Passive-Aggressive, Aggressive, and Assertive. These four aspects can either make one feel confident in their conversation or make one feel as though they're being bullied. By learning these definitions and understanding the tone to some of the examples, you will be able to listen to instances of friendly or unfriendly conversations.

How To Communicate Successfully

Below are some essential skills to help you make communication in the workplace successful:

Encourage More One-To-One Conversations And Phone Conversations

Today, people prefer written communication because they are used to writing texts and posting written content on various social media platforms. As a result, emails have become more popular in the workplace. However, if you are in a busy office and everyone decided to send you an email, you would have quite a large load f emails to go through, and responding to each would be equally tasking. The entire process would take up much of your valuable time too. However, if people switched to phone calls and one-on-one conversations, communication would be quicker and simpler.

1. Encourage Open Discussions

Encourage the people in your organization to speak their minds by letting them know that all they speak will be heard. Always remind them that their opinions matter. When people are encouraged to speak, and their feedback is received with respect, they feel appreciated and valued, and they take pride in being part of the organization.

1. Let The Discussions Be Meaningful

If all that is spoken about in your meetings is unnecessary and pointless, you will notice that the attendance will begin to dwindle. People begin to lose interest in the meetings and discussions because they perceive them as a waste of time. Too often, organizations hold meetings for the sake of it, just because the meeting is indicated on the regular schedule. This is not right. Meetings should be held only when necessary: other times, communicate your ideas and additional information through phone calls or face-to-face conversations.

If you find that a meeting is still necessary, maintain a tight time limit and stick to the agenda.

1. Get Visual Aids

Sometimes, words are not enough to express your point, and you will need a graphic or any other visual aid to help bring the point home. Use a photo, a picture, a graph, a meme, or a short video to help get your point across. Most people understand and respond better to visual information. They will also remember the visual aids for longer than they would if you only spoke some plain words.

1. Be Careful When Wording Emails

It is difficult to interpret the speaker's tone when communication is done via text. Through this media, your communication can go either way. It is not a wonder if the reader interprets in a context for which the writer did not intend. When this happens, people are bound to get offended unnecessarily just because they read the information in a particular way, even though it was not meant to be as such. This happens especially in situations where the writer has left room for interpretation by writing ambiguously. However, if you take caution and are clear about what you are talking about, no one will misinterpret you.

If you must communicate through written text, ensure that you proofread it to ensure that it delivers the tone that you meant it to. Also, confirm that you use the correct spelling, grammar, and punctuation as these too can be interpreted as rudeness and as being unprofessional.

1. Let Your Words Be Simple

The reality is that we are not all on the same footing when it comes to vocabulary. Therefore, to ensure that everyone understands what you say, use simple words. Ambiguous words only lead to misunderstanding and may require you to have to explain yourself better again, ultimately wasting your precious time.

1. Act Out The Message

It is not until you see someone do something, or you do it yourself, that the message behind it is completely absorbed. Words are easily forgotten, but deeds, not so much. Acting out what you would want your team to emulate is a very effective method of communication because, in the first place, you have demonstrated to them that what you want to be done is possible. Let the people see you do what you would want them to do, and they will be challenged to do it. There will be no excuses.

1. Avoid Repetition

If you want to be taken seriously, don't sound like a broken record. Don't keep repeating instructions or trying to beat them down with your words, into submission. Give your instructions just once, and ask if they are clear to everyone. If some have not understood, repeat your instructions, and when this is done, step aside and let your people go to work. Demand good results and make yourself busy. You will earn their respect this way, when they do not see you hovering over them all the time, repeating instructions they already heard.

How To Talk To Your Bosses

The thought of speaking to your boss can be quite frightening, especially when you need to talk to them about sensitive topics like salary increases, bonuses, some unfair terms at work, or about quitting your job. During these times, you often have minimal time to make your case, you nervously anticipate any follow-up questions, and you dread your boss' reaction.

Many times, the opportunities you get will also not be in your favor: you could be in an elevator, you could be asked into a meeting discussing something entirely different, or you could get your opportunity during a phone call. Speaking with your boss can be terrifying because your career is literally in your boss' hands, and most times, your boss' temperament, ego and predisposition will be different from yours. You also must remain true to yourself and not compromise on your values.

When it comes to speaking to your boss, there is always the risk that if you could wind up unemployed if you disagree with your employer. However, being a yes woman or man will do nothing for your personal and career growth. However, the following tips will help you remain safe while getting your voice across so that your issues are addressed, and working becomes easier.

Chapter 14:

EMOTIONAL AWARENESS/INTELLIGENCE

Intelligence is of different types, and it is important to understand each of them and how to use them in our daily lives. Intelligence is measured in quotients, and the most common type is the intelligence quotient or IQ. This refers to the ability to reason things out logically and memorize stuff. Another common type of intelligence is the curiosity quotient or CQ, which measures the ability to learn a new concept or subject. The third form is emotional intelligence, which we discuss extensively. In this chapter, you will learn about the definition, signs, and benefits of emotional
intelligence or EQ as it is popularly known.

Emotional intelligence was introduced by two researchers – Peter Salovey of Yale University and John Mayer of New Hampshire University. It refers to the ability to perceive, analyze, and influence a person's emotions and the emotions of others.

Emotional intelligence shows you how to use your intelligence in the right way. It helps you recognize, assess, and use your emotions correctly. In summary, it evaluates a person's emotional state.

Research shows that individuals who possess high EQ are always creative, result-oriented and succeed more in business than those with high IQ and low EQ. this is because emotional skills have been found to affect business performance more than technical skills.

Emotional Intelligence Model

In the 1990s, Peter Salovey and John Mayer devised an emotional intelligence model that can be used to define a person's ability to control emotions. These two researchers broke the model into four parts, namely:

- Self-awareness which is the ability to understand and acknowledge individual emotions
- Self-motivation which refers to the ability to stay focused on achieving set goals despite the level of impulsiveness and doubt
- Need management. This is the capability to handle emotions maturely based on the current situation
- Relationship management is the ability to handle disagreements and mediate between conflicting parties

This model indicates that if you are in total control of your emotions, you can easily control your reactions and actions. Through this, you can develop strong communication and social skills, and also be compassionate about others. Many researchers suggest that emotional intelligence is essential for leading a fulfilled life.

In summary, emotional intelligence comprises of two aspects

• Recognizing, analyzing and managing personal emotions

• Recognizing, analyzing and influencing other peoples' emotions

Emotional intelligence is mostly seen when a person is under pressure. It is measured using standardized psychometric tests. The result of these tests is referred to as the Emotional Quotient or EQ. Although the concept has been received with a lot of criticism, EQ has gained a lot of interest from the general public, especially in organizations. Most employers incorporate EQ in their search and selection processes, as well as in leadership training.

Importance of Emotional Intelligence

Although emotional intelligence is not as popular as IQ, research shows that emotional intelligence is one of the most important aspects when it comes to learning new ideas and skills. It has been found that the level of success in learning boils down to how a person can control their emotions and confidence. It is also affected by how well the learner is able to communicate, cooperate with the teacher, and manage their elatedness.

Several scientists have related emotional intelligence to organizational aspects such as individual and group performance, leadership, and change management. High emotional intelligence comes with several benefits. Here are some of them.

Improved Physical Health

Taking good care of our bodies impacts overall wellness and helps reduce stress levels. The ability to do this is largely influenced by our emotional intelligence. If you are aware of your emotional state, you will react to circumstances cautiously, and this can result in less worry and stress.

Mental Health

Emotional intelligence affects individual attitudes and motivation. Being self- aware helps to reduce anxiety since the person is able to overcome mood swings easily. High intelligence often translates to a positive mood and attitude. This means that the individual will generally live a happy life.

Better Relationships

Since high EQ helps you to manage your emotions, you will communicate your feelings more accurately without hurting others. It also helps you to connect with other people's emotions. Therefore you will easily understand how to talk, treat, and relate with them on a personal level. EQ also helps you to determine how to respond to people's needs and questions in a way that does not affect them negatively.

Resolves Conflicts

When you are able to understand the emotions of others, it is easier to settle disagreements as soon as they start. High EQ means high negotiation capability since the person is able to understand the needs of others.

Leads to Success

High EQ acts as internal motivation. It increases your level of confidence, reduces procrastination, and keeps you focused on the objectives of your assignments. It helps you to develop better support networks that can be useful where resilience is required to complete a task. EQ improves your ability to relay timely gratification, which directly impacts your success.

EQ Benefits for the Workplace

EQ enables you to control your emotions when in the workplace. In the old working setups, employees were not allowed to express their emotions at work. However, these days, most employers allow this at work since they have understood the benefit of allowing employees to express how they feel. This is where EQ comes in.

In most organizations, people are required to work in teams. EQ seeks to ensure that each team has a healthy environment to work in since it makes individuals aware of their emotions and the emotions of others. In most cases, people with high emotional intelligence tend to be more flexible and adaptable when it comes to working in teams.

Leaders who possess high EQ tend to raise happier subordinates. This automatically translates to higher productivity. Nowadays, companies higher candidates whose EQ is high enough to enable them to fit in the existing teams. As a result, most organizations incorporate EQ testing in the hiring process. Let us have a detailed look at the importance of emotional intelligence in the workplace.

Improved Team Performance

A team comprising of highly intelligent members is likely to produce the best results on an assignment. It is easy for such members to get along without disagreements, and since each is curious to learn, research becomes easy. The members will know how to communicate with each other. They will have confidence in each other, value each other's opinions, and respond to questions and suggestions positively. They also share ideas with ease and are less likely to dominate a situation without consulting others first. They are thoughtful and have the interest of the group at heart.

High Adaptability to Change

When introducing something new to an organization, most employees tend to resist it. Emotional intelligence equips employees with the ability to handle and deal with any form of change. It helps employees develop a positive attitude towards change items. Such employees can easily inspire other members of a team to embrace the new concept, idea, or process positively too.

The reason why high EQ individuals adapt to change easily because they are well prepared to handle anxiety, stress, and concerns without a struggle. They are, therefore, able to adjust more easily to new environments that suit the business.

Good Negotiation Skills

High emotional quotient allows you to engage in touch conversations within the organization. For example, you may encounter an angry customer or difficult employee that needs to be calmed down. In such circumstances, difficult conversations may arise, and with the right EQ, you can easily connect with the emotions of such people in an attempt to offer a solution to their issues. By using EQ in the workplace, it is very easy to control individual emotions and reach an agreement for each disagreement. Doing this creates a positive work environment that increases the motivation of employees and customers at large.

Networking

Emotional intelligence makes it possible for you to build trust around people. High EQ facilitates good communication since you are able to empathize with those around you. This is a key phenomenon for leaders who must build networks within and outside the organization. A great leader seeks to understand people in terms of how they work and what they need to stay motivated. This is essential for steering teams in the right direction.

Common Vision

As individuals spend the day at work, both positive and negative emotions may arise. In such circumstances, each person can apply emotional intelligence to demonstrate consistent behavior and communicate any challenges or strengths to the rest of the team. By doing this, the team can come up with a common vision for all the members since each of them is able to control their emotions and remain focused on the goal.

In most cases, individuals who are emotionally intelligent remain optimistic however difficult a work assignment gets. They have a mindset for growth and are able to endure all obstacles to ensure completion of a project. The motivation for such employees is not external – it comes from within. They derive their joy from completing work projects successfully. This means that emotionally intelligent employees will work extra hard and not give up easily. They measure their merit on how effective an assignment has been done, and it is important that organizations keep such employees motivated and happy.

Improved Communication

It is always difficult for people with low emotional intelligence to express themselves. Highly intelligent people connect with others with ease. They are able to earn respect from others and create lasting relationships within a short time span. They remain calm in case of challenges and easily accept input from others. Because of this, they can easily communicate and influence the behavior of others. This creates an environment for them to succeed within a short time.

Great Office Environment

Emotional intelligence boosts the morale of staff, creating a better office environment. Each organization desires that its many staff respect and get along with each other. Some organizations list this as one of the cultures, but sometimes it becomes difficult for employees to work together, especially if they have unresolved differences. A good office environment motivates employees to enjoy their work and also the people they are working with. As co-workers get along with each other, they will be able to discuss ideas and projects that can be of benefit to the organization. This creates a sense of belonging for each of them as they will be sure of each other's' support. Office managers are often given the responsibility of ensuring this happens by creating room, activities, and events that bring employees together.

Increased Self-Awareness

One great advantage of emotional intelligence is that it guides employees in understanding their strengths and weaknesses. Employees who have identified their development areas can easily accept feedback as well as positive criticism. Such can easily be convinced to improve in some of the areas they are weak in. Mostly, managers become defensive when offering feedback to employees. This can reduce the effectiveness through which the feedback is received, resulting in reduced productivity levels. It is also difficult to work with employees who do not understand their weaknesses. Managers can use EQ as a tool to make employees understand themselves better. Once the employees understand themselves, they will be able to view constructive criticism positively and beware of what they should do to improve on their performance.

High Self-Control

Just like in any other setup, the workplace can only thrive when employees are self-controlled. People with higher EQ understand how to handle tough circumstances and challenges. In any business setup, uncomfortable situations will always arise. This is especially common for people in leadership positions.

Tough circumstances may revolve around dealing with unhappy clients. These require you to remain positive and calm, even if the client is the one on the wrong. It could also be a supervisor that is angry with your work, and this can make you feel uneasy and unappreciated. The examples are many. High emotional intelligence helps you remain calm in such situations. It keeps you from emotional outbursts and any other unnecessary reactions. Individuals with high emotional quotient do understand that reacting negatively during tough occurrences only makes things worse. They are thus able to restrain themselves and only display their emotions when necessary.

Empathy and Compassion

This benefit is ideal both within and outside the workplace. EQ plays an important role in making you compassionate towards other people. The act of compassion allows you to connect with people on a personal level. It is of great benefit for an employer if his subordinates maintain compassion for each other and with the clients. For instance, a client may delay paying for a service or product because of an unfortunate circumstance. An employee can be compassionate enough to give the client more time to make the payment. Through this, the client becomes a loyal customer to the organization. However, an employee with low EQ may keep harassing the client due to the late payment. Eventually, the organization may lose the client.

Since leadership is all about making decisions, every leader must be able to show compassion in their daily activities. They must connect with employees and focus on improving their morale.

LEADERSHIP

Chapter 15:

HOW TO READ A FINANCIAL STATEMENT

This is stuff that your accountant will probably know backwards, but if you want to do business valuation properly, it doesn't hurt to have a feeling for the items that might be red flags, and to know where companies try to bury the bodies. Everything we've written in this chapter applies to all valuations, but it's particularly important for buyers.

For public companies that are listed on a stock exchange, you'll have extended data to look at. Even if you're not valuing that company, but using it as a comparison for the business you're looking at, it can be useful to read through the presentations to analysts (often on the website), and the discussion of operations at the front of the annual report. These may include additional industry-specific data, such as numbers of subscribers (for telecoms and pay-TV) or homes starts and completions (for housebuilders and developers), and can also sometimes flag up trends or new developments in the industry that you might have missed elsewhere.

Looking at the accounts is useless. Open a spreadsheet and start calculating the ratios. These will tell you far more about the business. There's a plethora of ratios you could use, but we'll highlight the ones that are most enlightening.

Days Sales Outstanding (Receivables / sales x 365). You need to look at the historic and industry comparisons. Does it look as if the company is having trouble getting paid? An increase in DSO might reflect lax credit terms, failure to pursue bad debts, or poor creditworthiness of customers - or it might reflect one big customer going to the wall. If you have access to management accounts, ask for a receivables aging report so you can see how long
customers are managing to extend their credit.

Inventory days (inventory / cost of goods sold x 365). Is stock turning over as fast as you'd expect it to? If stock turnover has been slowing down, is the product failing to compete, or are there other reasons, such as poor distribution? Again, if you have access to detailed figures, check to see exactly where the problem lies; a whole line of obsolete stock, or a downturn across the board? Remember to check for write-downs, which might temporarily make the position look better.

Borrowings - look back in the notes to the accounts for the *maturity profile*. That will show you any debt that has to be repaid and how long the business has till it needs to repay it - if there's a big debt that comes due shortly, beware! (Though of course, that just might mean the business is available at a bargain price - and if you have the funds to pay off the debt, you'll have made a great purchase.)

Look at the profit margins. You'll want to calculate gross margin (sales less cost of goods sold, as a percentage of sales) - this is particularly important for retailers, as it represents their direct costs - all other costs are fixed. If it's falling, it may indicate that the business can't pass on increased costs to its customers.

EBITDA margin is probably the most useful single ratio you can calculate. Take the pre-tax operating profit, and add back interest, and then the depreciation and amortisation (you'll find that in the notes, most likely). Calculate this figure as a percentage of sales turnover. It takes out debt and tax, takes out depreciation because it's a non-cash item, and basically shows you the cash profitability of the business.

Look at the return on assets. There are quite a few different ways to calculate this, that we won't go into here, but we particularly like to use EBITDA over total assets (that is, working capital plus fixed assets). It takes financing and tax out of the equation, and shows how efficiently the business is generating profit from the assets it holds - how much profit it's making for each dollar invested. The higher, the better, obviously!

When you're looking at the figures, you should also ask how that margin or return is being achieved. Are margins going up simply because the business is charging higher prices? That can boost returns for a while, but it might not be sustainable above a certain level, or customers will start to look elsewhere. Or does the business have a higher return on assets than comparable companies because it has a unique resource - a brewery that owns its own borehole for water, or a manufacturer that has designed its own high-specification production process for components and gained a cost advantage?

Sometimes being the dominant player in just one city can be a huge advantage. The local big player can afford to pay more for local advertising than national firms which don't have such a good foothold. Sometimes, local players pick off all the high margin business, leaving the big national firms, which are less nimble, to pick up the less profitable jobs. That's happened with parcels carriers and couriers, for instance.

Be suspicious if it looks as if cost cutting has boosted returns in the last couple of years. Cost cutting can also help increase margins in the short term, but eventually leaves the business with few options for margin growth - and sometimes with a less competitive product and a less motivated workforce.

Look out for changes in accounting practice. For instance, depreciation rates can be changed in order to charge less depreciation and thereby boost the operating profit figure.

One item you should always look for is related party transactions. Sales to associate companies, loans to directors, or purchases of shares in companies that are also significant customers, are all warning signs unless they can be properly explained to your satisfaction. (Loans to directors in smaller businesses are sometimes simply driven by tax efficiency.)

The relationship with the auditors is also worth watching. If a company has changed auditors once, that might be because they experienced poor customer service, or found another auditor would charge them significantly less for the same job. But if a company changes auditors twice within a few years, there might be a bit of a problem. Another thing to watch out for is a company that uses the same accountants as auditors, consultants, and to manage payroll and other functions - how independent is that audit going to be?

And look for sharp accounting practices. Despite tight audit requirements, there are still quite a few areas where companies can pick and choose their treatment of items. One we really hate is capitalisation of current costs. Normally, if you spend money wining and dining a customer, or leafleting potential customers, or buying TV ads, or pitching for business, that comes out of your current costs - it comes out of profit and loss account. But some cable TV companies decided their figures would look a whole lot better if they treated this as an investment, instead. The costs were put on the balance sheet as an asset, and so profits increased by the amount that *wasn't* written off. Many software companies, with rather more reason, capitalise some of their research and development costs.

Be very careful if you see this going on. It's

not *wrong* necessarily, but it's not the most conservative way of treating costs - and it also means the net book value has been inflated.

If you have ever looked at an annual report from a big company, you will have noticed how it splits into different sections. There are pretty pictures and (usually) optimistic words at the front, and then there is a boring black and white section with the numbers. There are numbers in the front section, too, but usually arranged in infographics, and selected to give the best impression.

If you want the truth, better look at the boring bits and do your own calculations – that is how great investors get to grips with the companies they invest in.

If you can grab an annual report to look at while you are using this book, you will make your life much easier – and you'll be learning from a real-world example, which will help you when you come to apply the lessons to your own business. You may be able to order one up from a major company or download a pdf from the Internet. It is easier to start on a manufacturing, services or retail business, like Intel, Microsoft or Amazon, rather than a bank or insurance company, as the latter has a specific type of business that is not so easy to understand.

There are three principal statements to looks at.

First, there is the profit and loss account – how much money the company is making.

Second, there is the balance sheet – what the company owns and what it owes.

And third, there is the cash flow account, and this adjusts the profits to show what cash actually came into and went out of the company.

Let's think of that in terms of a typical household:

The profit and loss account shows your salary coming in, your various bills being paid out, and what is left at the end of the month for savings.

The balance sheet shows the value of your car, house, designer handbags, Star Wars figurine collection, whatever – *less* the total of your mortgage, personal loans, and credit card balance.

The cash flow account adjusts the profit and loss

account to show actual cash in and out. For instance, if you buy a car for cash, your profit and loss account should show the depreciation on the car every month over its expected useful life, but the cash flow will show the actual purchase price in the month you buy it. The idea is that the profit and loss account smooths out investment decisions like buying a car or a factory – but the cash flow shows only cash.

The Profit and Loss Account

The profit and loss account is, in essence, a series of subtractions. We start with the revenue of the business – its total sales (or rents, or royalties) – and then we subtract the costs to arrive at the profit.

We so often talk in generic terms about 'making a profit' or 'the company's profits', but one of the things we need to think about is that there are several levels of profit.

There is *gross profit* – that is a return on materials cost before you take any other costs (like premises, staff or finance) into account. Retailers work on gross margin – or invert the ratio to work on 'markup'. They buy a crate of apples at $45 and need to sell at, say, a 100% markup, or $90. You *can* also look at gross profit in services – if you are selling billable hours. It is the difference between what you pay your staff and what you sell their time for (though you would need to exclude non-billable hours and support staff from the equation).

If you look at all the operating costs of a business, including the premises costs (rent, electricity, depreciation of machinery, etc.), support staff, professional fees, and so on, what you get when you subtract them from the revenues of the business is the *operating profit*. It is a good level at which to look at the profitability of operations overall, as it doesn't matter whether your business is entirely equity funded, or financed mainly by bank loans – the operating profit will be the same.

Next, we subtract the financial costs of the business. So if you have any bank loans or mortgages, this is where you take out the servicing cost for the period that we are looking at, whether it is a month, quarter or year. All the interest paid is subtracted (and if you are lucky enough to have a pot of cash, of course, it is added back in). Here we have *pre-tax profit*.

Next, we take out tax. In a perfect world, it would be the tax rate times the pre-tax profit – but because the tax department has different rules about what is an allowable expense from the accountants, it will often differ a bit from what you would expect. *Post-tax profit* is profit free and clear, and now you can decide what to do with it. If you are a one-person business, it is all yours; if you're running a company, you have to decide whether to pay a dividend to shareholders.

Take out the dividend, or whatever you took out for yourself, and what you have left is *retained profit* – the profit for the year that is left in the business to fund future investment. Some businesses keep all the profit – that is a good decision if you know you can invest at a rate of return higher than the bank pays on cash. For instance, if you are in a fast-growing business. That is why many tech companies don't pay dividends.

Remember we talked about how the profit and loss account is different from the cash flow? One big item that is different is *amortization and depreciation.* When you buy a long-term business asset, you estimate how long it will last – a computer might last three years, a major piece of manufacturing equipment twenty years. If you are going to use a bread oven for 15 years, then you say 'Okay, every year I'm going to use 1/15 of the oven, so to speak, so I'm going to match the 1/15 of the cost of the oven with the revenues each year to find my profit' – in accountant-speak, you amortize the cost over 15 years (you might also reckon that if you are likely to sell the oven for scrap at the end, you should take the scrap value as a *residual value*... but that is a level of detail we don't need to worry about). Anyway, we might want to add back that depreciation and amortization. The difference? Depreciation is on physical objects, amortization on intangibles, like goodwill and software. We will add it back to get a better idea of the cash profit that the business is making – and we add it back to the operating profit to get EBITDA, earnings before interest, tax, depreciation, and amortization. That is a great number that a lot of businesses use for benchmarking because however a business is funded, and whatever its asset base, EBITDA will compare well across the industry. (Besides, one firm might think your bread oven's only good for ten years – so for every $100 you charge in depreciation, that firm would be charging $150. Suppose you had the same revenues and the same costs, apart from depreciation – that company would look less profitable on every measure except for EBITDA, which would be exactly the same.)

The Balance Sheet

Where the profit and loss account works on the basis of subtraction, the balance sheet is about addition. You add up all the assets of the business – the things you own. Then you add up all the liabilities of the business – things you owe to others (that includes bank loans, but also services you have to provide for which you've already been paid, trade invoices you haven't paid, and a provision for tax you will pay next year on profit you made this year). Each side of the balance sheet should balance – that's how it gets its name.

But why does it balance?

Let's just think about a very simple business. Suppose you kick off with $100 in cash which you decide to invest in setting up a little crafts business selling on Etsy. You spend $50 on a sewing machine and $20 on textiles, and then you make some nice tote bags. Your balance sheet has one liability – $100 that is owed to you, in shareholder's equity; and it has three assets – the sewing machine, the cloth, and $30 in cash. That is why it balances.

You sell all of your original stock for $50, and for the sake of simplicity, we are going to decide you don't pay yourself anything. So now your asset side shows $50 for a sewing machine, no textiles (all gone), and $80 in cash – the $30 you had, and the $50 that customers paid. That is $130 against the original $100.

However, you have made a profit, don't forget – $50 less the $20 you paid for the cloth. That profit belongs to shareholders (let's ignore tax for the moment), that is, to you – so you have to add it to the liabilities side of the balance sheet. $100 plus the $30 profit equals $130, and hey presto, both sides of the balance sheet balance, all over again.

Suppose you decide to borrow $100 from the bank. Now you have $230 on the liabilities side, consisting of $130 in equity and retained profit plus $100 debt. But the money you have borrowed will sit on the assets side as $100 cash, or as the value of whatever assets you've bought with the money. So, again, the balance sheet balances.

The balance sheet is useful for looking at the business' resources, both physical and financial. For instance, you can look at the tangible assets – how much money have you invested? And how productively is it being put to use? How much stock or work in progress have you got?

You can also look at your sources of funding – how much is debt? How much is equity? How much retained profit do you have? (that is the amount that you can distribute in dividends, so it is a more important number than it might seem).

You can look at the balance between long-term and

short-term assets, and whether your funding sources match it – if you have a lot of long-term assets, but your financing is all short-term (like an overdraft), you might want to think about restructuring your balance sheet.

We are going to look at the ratios that can help you analyze these statements further in a later chapter. For now, just get happy with the format of these accounts and, if you like, track down the detail in the notes to the accounts, which will show you what has gone into each overall category.

Actually, the notes to the accounts are where real finance nerds get their fun. Very, very occasionally you might find that the numbers don't add up! Over the years, analysts have found various bodies buried in the notes:

An investment in shares in a company that then became a client and bought its shareholder's software – they couldn't get customers any other way!

A big leasing company that looked as if it was making loads of profit – but if you did the cash flow sums correctly, was hemorrhaging cash.

A company that was capitalizing all its marketing costs, 'saving' millions a year.

A company that everyone thought was a house builder, but when you looked at the detailed breakdowns of revenue, made more money trading building plots.

The use of special purpose vehicles to hide huge amounts of debt (Enron).

Large payments to directors of the company including loans to directors which were never repaid.

Special purpose vehicles used to create paper profits when the parent company 'sold' them supplies or charged them interest on loans.

Some pieces of creative accounting don't come to light until the company crashes and burns. However, other pieces of creative accounting are there to see – if you trawl deep enough.

You may not, right now, be up to it, but you can get an idea of what goes on by reading *The Smartest Guys in the Room* or *Conspiracy of Fools* (about Enron), or *The Big Short* (about the sub-prime mortgage bubble, though this is more finance markets than company finance), or *Final*

Accounting (Arthur Andersen, the accountancy firm that fell apart after its role in the Enron collapse came to light).

Chapter 16:

HOW INCOME TAXES WORKS

Taxes are involuntary charges imposed on individuals or companies and imposed by a government entity — whether local, regional or national — to fund the government's operations. In economics, taxes are levied on whoever bears the tax burden, whether that is the taxable person, such as a company, or the end-users of the business's products.

Understanding Taxation

The government generally taxes its individual, corporate citizens to help finance public works, services, construct and maintain the infrastructures used in a country. The tax collected is used to boost the economy and all those who work in it. Taxes are applied in the U.S. and many other countries around the world to some form of money a taxpayer receives. The money may be income gained from wages, capital gains from the growth of assets, dividends obtained as taxable revenue, payment for goods and services, etc.

A percentage of the taxpayer's income or revenue is taken and passed to the government. Paying taxes at rates set by the state is compulsory. Tax avoidance — the intentional failure to pay one's full tax obligations — is punishable by statute. Many governments use an agency or department to collect taxes; the Internal Revenue Service (IRS) performs this function in the United States.

There are several forms of tax which are very common:

- **Income Tax:** A percentage of earnings deposited with the federal government
- **Corporate tax:** A percentage of corporate income that the government collects as revenue to finance federal programs
- **Sales tax:** On income-duties on other products and services
- **Property tax:** Based on the valuation of the house and land properties
- **Tariff:** Taxes levied on manufactured products to improve internal businesses
- **Estate tax:** The rate charged at the time of death to the fair market value of the land in the property of an individual

Tax systems differ widely among nations. Before earning income or making business there, individuals and companies need to research a new locale's tax laws carefully.

How Income Taxes Functions

Taxes are applied according to some variables, including the taxpayer's filing status—married filing jointly, married filing separately, single filing, or household heading. What rank an individual has can make a big difference in how much they're taxed.

A taxpayer's source of revenue also creates a difference in taxes. It is important to understand the vocabulary of the various forms of income and other factors affecting how income is paid. Learning this information helps taxpayers to plan their budgets at their actual net profit for the best result.

Techniques that can help involve annual tax-loss harvesting to balance investment gains with investment losses and property planning work to shield hereditary wealth for heritages.

Small businesses measure their income tax profit or loss, then include the information on their tax returns. This guide will help you decide which forms to use and how to compile for those forms of information.

This guide is for small companies filing their tax returns alongside their returns on Schedule C (Form 1040). It includes sole proprietors and control of a single-member LLC. If your company is a corporation or an S corporation, check out the *Full Guide for Companies and S Corporations.* Whether your company is a multi-owner LLC or a partnership, here's a Guide to Partnership Business Tax.

Due Dates

Small businesses file their corporate tax returns alongside their returns; the due date is the same as personal income tax returns: April 15. If the due date falls on a holiday or weekend, then the year's due date is the next business day.

Schedule C Income Tax Forms

Here are the requisite forms for or sole proprietors and single-member LLCs, including the forms needed to measure self-employment tax:
- Schedule C
- Schedule C Instructions
- Schedule S.E. for self-employment tax
- Schedule S.E. instructions

Tax Information Needed to Complete Schedule C

The details you may need to fill out Schedule C:
- Details to measure the cost of the goods sold, whether the inventory of items or parts for sale is available
- Documentation to show all corporate tax deductions from company travel expenses, commuting expenses, and work meals (entertainment expenses are no longer deductible as business expenses)
- Cost information to measure depreciation expenses for the acquisition of company properties such as cars and equipment

• Provide some details on your home's business usage if you work from home for a deduction for home business space.

Self- Employment Taxes

Small business owners are forced to pay self-employment taxes (Social Security/Medicare taxes) on their corporate net income (profit). You don't have to pay self-employment tax if you don't have any business income during the year if your salary is $400 or less for the year.

A concise description of how tax is measured on self-employment:

• Bring net profit into your company

• Multiply the profit by 92.35% (0.9235)

• Multiply this number by 15.3 % (the tax rate for self-employment) to receive the sum of the self-employment tax.

• This number is used to determine your annual eligibility for Social Security/Medicare benefits.

• To lower your adjusted gross income for the year, you will subtract one- half of the self-employment tax.

• A tax software program or a tax preparer can measure the tax for you. Also, you can use Schedule S.E. to run the calculation yourself.

Paying Taxes

Your company will have to fulfill its federal, state, and local tax responsibilities if it is to stay in good legal standing. The nature and location of your company will determine the taxes your business has to pay.

Determine Your Tax Responsibilities in the State

Your company may have to pay both local and state taxes. Tax laws vary by location and structure of the business, so you'll need to check with local and state governments to know your business's tax obligations.

In small businesses, the two most common categories of state and local tax requirements are payroll taxes and job taxes.

The nature of your company defines your **State** income tax obligations. For example, corporations are taxed separately from the owners when single owners record their personal and company income taxes using the same form.

If you have workers in your company, you will be responsible for paying taxes on **State** jobs. They vary by state and include workers' compensation benefits, taxes on unemployment insurance, and emergency disability for disabilities. You will also be responsible for withholding the income tax on workers. To find out how much you need to deduct and when you need to give it to the IRS, consult with your local tax authority.

Decide Your Income Tax Obligations

The nature of your company defines what federal taxes you have to pay, and how you pay them. Some of the taxes require payment all year round, so it's important to know your tax obligations before your tax year ends.

Tax on self employ Tax Calculation Tax on employers Excise tax

The business tax category may have special rules, requirements, or IRS forms that you need to fold. Consult with IRS to see which company taxes are appropriate for you.

If your business has employees, you may need to deduct taxes from their paychecks. Federal job taxes include payroll taxes, social security and medicare taxes, unemployment, and taxes on self-employment. Check with the IRS to find out what taxes you need to subtract.

How to Save Taxes

One of the first questions you need to determine is whether you need to get a professional's help to handle your corporate taxes — and help you plan so you can take advantage of certain deductions. "I'm also asked how to decide when to speak to a doctor, and there are two ways to get things done," says Colombia. "One way is to look at the tax and determine if it would cost me less to talk to a specialist than to pay my tax bill. Otherwise, think that if you don't pay a lot of tax in that field now, but you know you're going to be in the future, you should figure out whether there's a way to invest properly."

Growing Forms of Saving on Tax

You will benefit from certain regular tax laws, which will save your business money. Here are just a few examples:

Contribute to a Pension Program.

When your company is successful, you will shield income in a covered pension fund that will provide you with a tax benefit for your investments.

Delay tax on investment earnings (tax is eventually charged when you start withdrawing money from the program, usually at retirement), says Weltman. If you have employees, you will earn employee loyalty and provide them with an opportunity to save for retirement.

Adopt an "accountable program."

If you have employees and reimburse them for corporate use of their cars, adopt an accountable program to save them and save the company's payroll tax, Weltman says. This arrangement allows you to reimburse an employee for business expenses without treating them with the reimbursements as revenue.

Defer tax and expedite deductions.

There are some steps you can take to push off taxes into the next tax year by the end of the year and raise your deductions in the current tax year. "Take your bills out a few days later in the last month of the year," Colombia says. That means getting paid in

January of the next year a few days later and being able to defer the income, rather than being paid in December of the current year and having to declare that income immediately. Likewise, one way to speed up your deductions is to see what debts you owe in January and pay them by the end of December so that you can take the deduction in the current year, says Colombia.

Design your company appropriately. Colombia says this is the "single most neglected part of tax planning." Most small start-ups don't change their business structure when they need it. For example, if you have a closely held company in which you, the owner, receive the income, these are usually set up as an LLC or an S corporation. However, there is nothing wrong with such arrangements; you will be able to achieve tax benefits by structuring your business as a C corporation, where the first $50,000 of your profits is taxed at a rate of 15 % compared to a rate of 35 % if you are in the highest tax bracket, he says.

Conclusion

In this book you have found the 16 things school doesn't teach you. It is essential today to be surrounded by the most total and boundless knowledge. This book surrounds you with technical and motivational, scientific and statistical, mental and cognitive information.

A lot of people take part in their passion hoping it is going to bring them material results. When this fails to occur, the passion could minimize or perhaps even be forgotten. Don't be bitter if achievement fails to accompany passion.

Some individuals are responsible for neglecting themselves. They are too active with the career, business, relationship or family life. Doing the thing you like during a necessary break is helpful to your well-being. It is going to result in a far more relaxed & happier you. It is the greatest remedy for stress. Managing stress creates a far more sensible and fulfilled existence.

Often people are frustrated to pursue passion due to destructive criticisms. These criticisms can come from other individuals or from their own self. Individuals might not like the writing style, the singing or even what you cook.

Now take a path of greater awareness, for knowledge is power. Nothing else matters.

CPSIA information can be obtained
at www.ICGtesting.com
Printed in the USA
BVHW091048040121
596933BV00013B/1072